Half Brain Management Techniques

Dr. Isola O. Busuyi

TABLE OF CONTENTS

INTRODUCTION..10

Managerial Decision Making..............11

Effective Decision Making..............15

Decision Making and Cultures..........30

Chinese Decision Making................33

Intuition...34

Historical Overview............................36

Intuition and Business.................37

Intuition and gender....................40

Country of Operation...................47

Intuition, Gender, Country of Operation and Decision Making................76

MANAGEMENT LEVEL AND BRAIN USAGE 98

EXPERIENCE AND BRAIN USAGE 119

SEX AND BRAIN USAGE......................... 140

BRAIN USAGE AND COUNTRY OF OPERATION 164

SUMMARY, CONCLUSIONS AND RECOMMENDATION. 222

REFERENCES CITED 225

Appendix A: Intuitive Skill Survey..238

Appendix B: Permission Letter to Use AIM Survey..240

LIST OF TABLES

TABLE 1 99

TABLE 2 102

TABLE 3 105

TABLE 4 108

TABLE 5 111

TABLE 6 114

TABLE 7 117

TABLE 8 120

TABLE 9 123

TABLE 10 126

TABLE 11 129

TABLE 12 132

TABLE 13 135

TABLE 14 138

TABLE 15 141

TABLE 16 144

TABLE 17 147

TABLE 18 150

TABLE 19 153

TABLE 20...156

TABLE 21...159

TABLE 22...162

TABLE 23...166

TABLE 24...169

TABLE 25...172

TABLE 26...175

TABLE 27...178

TABLE 28...181

TABLE 29...184

TABLE 30...187

TABLE 31...190

TABLE 32...193

TABLE 33...196

TABLE 34...199

TABLE 35...202

TABLE 36...205

TABLE 37...208

TABLE 38...211

TABLE 39...214

TABLE 40...217

TABLE 41...220

LIST OF FIGURES

FIGURE 1 100

FIGURE 2 103

FIGURE 3 106

FIGURE 4 109

FIGURE 5 112

FIGURE 6 115

FIGURE 7 118

FIGURE 8 121

FIGURE 9 124

FIGURE 10 127

FIGURE 11 130

FIGURE 12 133

FIGURE 13 136

FIGURE 14 139

FIGURE 15 142

FIGURE 16 145

FIGURE 17 148

FIGURE 18 151

FIGURE 19 154

FIGURE 20 157

FIGURE 21 160

FIGURE 22 163

FIGURE 23 167

FIGURE 24 170

FIGURE 25 173

FIGURE 26 176

FIGURE 27 179

FIGURE 28 182

FIGURE 29 185

FIGURE 30 188

FIGURE 31 191

FIGURE 32 194

FIGURE 33 197

FIGURE 34 200

FIGURE 35 203

FIGURE 36 206

FIGURE 37 209

FIGURE 38 212

FIGURE 39 215

FIGURE 40 218

FIGURE 41 221

INTRODUCTION

In a speech delivered on Tuesday, August 31st, 2010 President Barrack Obama reiterated the importance of innovation to US economy. He said "America still lead the world in innovation" The problem however is that business schools are reluctant to teach right brain management skills. Business schools continue to emphasize left brain rational decision making without referencing right brain intuitive management decision making techniques. This in essence has led to what is referred to in this book as half brain management education.

The concept of using intuition in managerial decision making is still not as popular as one would expect. "Twenty-four texts, prepared for courses in Principles of Management and published between 1974 and 1977, were examined in order to learn about the attention they gave to intuition. Only three of them had any information about intuition (Isaack, 1978)" An examination of seven management textbooks written between 2000 and 2006 by this researcher did not find any significant material on intuition in any of the books. This is despite the fact that several studies in recent past have led to more discussion on intuitive decision making. In a recent study, Church (2005) found fifty-four publications that reported empirical studies centered on intuition.

Managerial Decision Making

Decision making is the process of choosing a course of action among alternatives (Hodgetts, 2006). In defining management, Mintbzerg (1973) saw decision making as one of the three major managerial roles. Mintzberg's definition of management was influenced by his intensive study of five CEOs and their organizations. Earlier management scholars had approached the subject differently although they all agree with the fact that management involves decision making. Mary Parker Follett (1917), defined management as "the art of getting things done through people" while Henri Fayol (1949) saw management as planning, organizing, leading, coordinating and controlling. The ten managerial roles identified by Mintbzerg were further classified into interpersonal, informational and decisional roles.

Interpersonal roles identified by Mintbzerg include figurehead, leader and liaison activities. As figureheads, managers operate as symbolic heads of their units; they are expected to perform certain ceremonies, handle certain requests and represent their units at social functions. As leaders, managers are responsible for motivating and training their subordinates. In the liaison role, the manager interacts with peers and people outside the organization.

Informational roles include monitor, disseminator and spokesperson roles. The interpersonal roles of managers prepare them for this unique role. As they interact with insiders and outsiders, they gain access to information needed to run the organization. In the monitor role, the manager receives and collects information. In the role of disseminator, the manager transmits special information into the organization. In the role of spokesperson, the manager disseminates the organization's information into its environment (Allen, 1998).

Decisional roles include entrepreneur, disturbance handler, resources allocator, and negotiator roles. The managers in their entrepreneurial roles are expected to initiate changes that can be controlled by their units. As disturbance handlers, managers are expected to handle threats facing their units. As resource allocators, managers decide on how organizations' resources are used. They make decisions on how physical, financial and human resources are allocated. The negotiator role demands that managers represent their units in all important negotiations.

Effective Decision Making

Decision making is necessitated by the existence of problems. In tackling the question of how decision should be made, early management writers put forward the rational decision making model. Peter Drucker (1967) widely acclaimed as the father of modern management, identified six major steps that should be followed by executives making decisions for their companies. In 2004, he presented another paper that further narrowed the whole process to three steps. The first step of the new approach focused on getting the needed knowledge while the remaining two steps focused on planning and acting. The six steps identified by the 1967 paper are classifying the problem, defining the problem, specifying the answer to the problem, deciding what is right, defining the actions needed to carry out decisions and testing the validity and effectiveness of decisions against actual course of events.

Classifying problems helps executives manage their time properly as time is one of the most critical resources available to executives. Drucker identified four different classes of problems which are internally generic problems, problems that are unique to the company but generic to the industry, truly exceptional problems and new generic problems. The author advised executives to use established rules to solve all generic problems while giving needed attention to truly unique problems.

Once classified, Drucker suggested that executives should then define the problem. Defining the problem involves identifying the key to solving the problem. Drucker (1967) said the most crucial aspect of problem definition is that it must be complete and continuous. Definitions must be checked against observable facts to ensure they are still valid. When they cease to be valid, new definitions must be developed.

Specifying what the decision has to accomplish is the next step. This is also is a dynamic process according to Drucker, when needs change, specifications must also change. Once the specifications are clearly stated, the effective executive can then select the right decision. Drucker suggested that this step must always start with the right decision since compromise can then be made later. When it is time to move from the right decision to the acceptable one, he advised executives to remember the difference between the usefulness of half loaf and the uselessness of half a child.

The fifth step in decision making involves converting the final decision to action.

Drucker said the conversion involves asking such questions as who needs to know about the decision. What actions need to be taken, who is to take the action? And how can the action be adapted to the capabilities of those responsible for taking it. The step would even involve putting the right incentives in place.

Information monitoring and reporting is the final stage of the decision making process identified by Drucker in his 1967 paper. At this stage, he suggested that executives should not rely solely on reports since they are only abstracts of reality. He said they should actually go where the action is taking place and observe for themselves. If the decisions are not working, he suggested quick revisions at the right time.

In his 2004 paper, Drucker (2004) saw effective decision making as a three stage process which starts with getting the needed knowledge and end with taking action after developing plans. The knowledge accumulating stage involves asking what needs to be done. He differentiated this question from that of what do I need to do? Starting from what needs to be done, the effective executive then selects one or two that are best done by him/her for further attention. The remaining tasks are delegated to others competent enough to handle them. This stage also requires continuous attention; Drucker said effective executives would often ask the question again once the first task is completed rather than just jumping to the next item on the list because the environment does change.

The planning stage starts by asking questions such as what does the company expect from the executive over the next few months- covering about two years in some cases. The process also involves asking which of the expectations, the executive wants to commit to and with what deadlines. The plan is supposed to be a statement of intention rather than a straight jacket. The plan would also create ways of checking results against plans and it then becomes the basis for managing the executive' s time.

The final step of the decision making process in the new paper is taking action. Taking action according to Drucker involves making people know the name of the person accountable for carrying out the plan, the deadline, the names of people who would be affected by the decision, and the names of people who would have to be informed about it. The actions must also be reviewed and non-performing decisions revised. The executive should also take responsibility for communications making sure he gets the type of information he needs the way it is needed.

Drucker also advised the executive to focus on opportunities and not on problems. He suggested that executives should make meetings productive and ensure that they think and say we at all times.

The rational decision model is predicated on six assumptions. Some of these assumptions rarely hold true in real life situations. The model assumes that the problem being solved is clear and that the decision maker has complete information regarding the decision. It also assumes that the decision maker can identify all the relevant criteria and list all the viable alternatives (Robbins & Judge, 2007). The rational decision model also assumes that the criteria and alternatives can be ranked and weighted to reflect their importance. The model assumes that the specific decision criteria are constant and that the weights assigned to them are stable over time. It is also assumed that the rational decision maker can obtain full information about criteria and alternatives thereby ignoring the impact of time or cost constraints. It is also assumed that rational decision maker will choose the alternative that yields the highest perceived value.

The ability to produce useful and novel ideas is one of the desirable elements of decision making. The rational model did not provide any means of producing creative ideas. This along with a few other almost impractical aspects of the rational model is what some refer to as the reason for satisfying by many decision makers. The rational model is an optimizing model but the impracticality of some of its assumptions makes many decision makers settle for bounded rationality. In bounded rationality, decision makers try to rationalize within the confines of the more simplified models of real life problems they build for themselves. Decision makers capture essential features of problems instead of capturing all its complex elements because of real life time pressures and the dynamics of the decision environment.

The in-exhaustive nature of bounded rationality has been found to leave room for systematic biases and errors (Robbins & Judge, 2007). Overconfidence bias occurs when decision makers are significantly higher in the correctness of their decisions than the decisions turn out to be. Studies show that overconfidence bias tends to reduce with increase in decision maker' s knowledge of their jobs. Anchoring bias is the tendency to fixate on initial information. Confirmation bias is selectively seeking out information that confirms decision makers' preconceived views. Availability bias is the tendency to base judgments on information that is readily available. Randomness error is the tendency to believe one can predict the outcome of random events. Representative bias and hindsight bias are some of the remaining myriads of systematic biases that can impair the quality of decisions made through bounded rationality.

In his 1967 paper, Drucker said effective managers are not overly concerned about speed of decisions; they take their time to consider all the variables and make sure they make the right decisions for the company. Critics of this approach to effective decision making refers to it as "analysis paralysis" Livingston (1971) claimed: Instruction in problem solving and decision making all too often leads to 'analysis paralysis' because managerial aspirants are required only to explain and defend their reasoning, not to carry out their decisions or even to plan realistically for their implementation. Chris Argyris (1973) published an analysis of *rational-man* theories in the *Public Administration Review* where he too, discussed the danger of over rationalization.

Douglas Dean and John Mihalasky (1974) discovered through their ten year research that executives whose companies increased the most profits, scored higher on tests of precognition than average. They tested approximately 165 CEOs and presidents of companies in the United States and found that 80% of the leaders who doubled or nearly doubled their profits in a five-year period had above-average scores on intuitive ability (Church, 2005). The findings of their research showed that intuitive managers were more successful than their more analytical counterparts. Studies by Agor (1989) also showed that top executives rated significantly higher than middle or low level managers in intuitive abilities. Agor was of the opinion that intuition can be regarded as distilled knowledge.

Isenberg (1984) also found out that Eighty percent of the senior managers he studied preferred using intuition in their decision making processes. He discovered that most successful managers do not follow the classical rational decision making process (Church, 2005). Isenberg discovered that successful managers do not try to solve one problem at a time; they just have overriding concerns that guides them in making decisions. Isenberg found out that most senior managers thought they were the only ones using intuition and that they were wrong in doing so. This tendency to conceal the use of intuition in decision making by managers is in line with the findings of Agor (1989), Maslow (1974), and Mintbzerg (1976). Isenberg (1984) saw intuition as distilled rationality.

Cappon (1993) tested over 3000 individuals and found out that women did not have more intuition than men. He believed that everyone had intuition and that it could be developed in individuals (Fields, 2001). Capon's request to administer his research instrument was turned down by many intuition-sensitive companies but companies in the manufacturing industry were quite receptive to his request. This might have skewed his findings. In approaching the study, his hypothesis was intuition is the secret to success in most endeavors. Cappon was a medical doctor and psychotherapist.

Parikh's (1994) global study of 1300 managers from Austria, Brazil, France, India, Japan, Netherlands, Sweden, United Kingdom, and the United States showed that managers used intuition successfully in business and personal settings. He reported that Managers found intuition especially useful in planning, marketing, public relations, human resource development, and research and development.

Klein's (2004) research in the 1990s with law enforcement, fire fighters, and the United States Marine Corp showed that intuition is utilized by typically male dominant professions. His discoveries indicated that, in emergency situations, the rational model was not used, rather a nonlinear approach was used that included intuition (Church, 2005). Klein asserted that intuition could be learned and developed in individuals.

Rosanoff (1991, 1999) wrote a nonacademic book on how to develop intuition. The guide discussed how intuition could be beneficial and useful in crisis situations, financial, business, and romantic relationships

(Church, 2005). Rosanoff's (1999) article for nurses identified ways to develop intuitive power and wisdom:

(a) Ask: before making any decision, stop and ask yourself how you really feel about what you are about to do,

(b) Be attentive: intuitive insight is often the first impression that occurs when faced with a new situation,

(c) Keep track: begin an intuition journal by jotting down your intuitive impressions and tracking your results,

(d) use power moments: begin team meetings by asking everyone to take a moment of silence to collect their thoughts about the meeting's agenda and write down a few personal thoughts, experiences, and feelings as they occur,

(e) nonanalytic thinking: stimulate nonanalytic impressions by having some toys in the center of the meeting table,

(f) force a decision: before all the data are assessed and discussed, ask team

members to state the decision they would make if they had to do so right now,

(g) keep journals: distribute small notebooks to team members and ask that they record stray thoughts, dreams, impressions, details, insignificant events that surround the project, and intuitions,

(h) the unpopular idea: ask team members what the "unpopular" information or choice is about a current project or situation, and

(i) Reflect: encourage reflective and creative breaks (pp. 160 – 161)

Decision Making and Cultures

In his 1974 seminal work titled *Management: Tasks, Responsibilities, Practices,* Drucker compared Japanese decision making to Western decision making. Drucker (1993) saw the entire Japanese decision making process as highly standardized and effective. In making decisions the Japanese debates proposed decision throughout the organization until a consensus is reached. During the organization wide discussion the Japanese are usually focused on defining the question rather than finding an answer as it is done in the West. They try to ensure that the whole organization agree on what the problem is. Once this consensus is reached it becomes easy to develop an answer. The top management then refers the decision to the appropriate people. The decision stage is called the "action stage". The choice of the appropriate group is often determined by manager's position on various issues revealed during the debate. The choice is, therefore, considered by some as actually picking the answer. Drucker saw similarities between the referral process and the practice of delegating certain decision making powers to political committees in the West.

In contrasting Japanese decision making process to the Western process Drucker said, the speed gained in making decisions, is usually lost during the process of selling the decision to other members of the organization who in some cases end up sabotaging the decision made. The rigorous groupthink process employed by the Japanese makes resistance to final decisions almost superfluous. Drucker also commented on the speed at which implementation of decisions progress in Japan at the "action stage". He said it could take the Japanese three years to finally agree that they need to license a product but once that decision is made it could take them less than three weeks to set up the factory needed to manufacture the product. Another observed advantage of the Japanese decision- making process is that it forces them to make only big decisions unlike in the West where Drucker said too much time is spent on small decisions. The Japanese decision making process also allow dissenting opinions to be voiced during the discovery process since the process does not start with preconceived answers.

Chinese Decision Making

Harmony with the environment is one of the central teachings of Confucius. The implication of this approach is far reaching in managerial decision making amongst the Chinese. Using Hofstede' s cultural universals further discussed later in this chapter, Dietrich (2003) concluded that the nation' s high score on power distance imply that participation in decision making is not highly esteemed by the Chinese. Deference to higher powers also implies less interest in participating in decision making. Harmony with the environment also implies less interest in subduing the environment. This could imply that decisions are often based on intuition and past experience. Consequently the Chinese tend to make less use of extensive data analysis (Martinsons and Westwood, 1997). Group orientation fostered by years of communism and Confucius teachings also promotes group decision making. Guanxi networks may also limit information flow. Face saving; an integral part of Chinese culture also promote deference as Chinese decision maker try to avoid losing face for making wrong decisions. High context nature of the Chinese culture moderates the need for and the use of computer-based information systems.

Intuition

Intuition has been defined by many scholars in various ways. Jung (1924) defined intuition as that psychological function which transmits perception in an unconscious way. In commenting on the diversity of definitions, Isaack (1978) wrote "an examination of the literature on intuition disclosed that authorities on the subject had different concepts about it" Behling & Eckel (1991) found eighty-seven descriptions of intuition during a search of two electronic data bases in twenty-four books and articles published between 1976 and 1987. In trying to make sense out of the descriptions, they recruited six MBA students to group the descriptions. Six clusters eventually emerged.

In one cluster, authors described intuition as a paranormal phenomenon. Top managers who relied on psychics to make decisions were cited as examples in this cluster. "H. L. Hunt relied on a psychic to help pick oil properties (Rowen, 1986)" A second cluster consists of descriptions of Intuition as a personality trait. Scholars in this category saw intuitive decision making as genetic or acquired very early in life (Behling & Eckel, 1991). Three of the remaining four clusters described intuition as an unconscious process, a set of actions, and distilled experience. The fourth cluster was named the residual category. Authors in this category defined intuition as decisions not made using the rational decision making process.

Historical Overview

Tracing the history of intuition can be quite challenging because of the various descriptions given the subject by various scholars. Using the paranormal approach to intuition, references to intuition can be found in the Old Testament. In 2 Kings Chapter 6, Elisha the prophet informed the king about plots to kill him through extra sensory knowledge, thereby saving the king' s life several times (KJV, 18:17). Some of the early writings on intuition came from philosophers such as Plato, Aristotle, and Kant (Church, 1991). Their writings on intuition were focused on whether the phenomenon was priori or posteriori.

Intuition and Business

The primary scholars in this section include Agor, Argyris, Barnard, Simon, and Westcott (Church, 2005). The first to write about intuition and its' use in the workplace was Chester Barnard (1938/1968) in his germinal work for managers, *The Functions of the Executive.* Chester Barnard (1938/1968) identified differences in mental processes and classified them as logical and non-logical mental processes. Logical mental processes were defined as conscious thinking which can be expressed in words or reasoning and non-logical mental processes as those not capable of being expressed in words (Simon, 1987). Barnard believed that both logical and non-logical was necessary for the success of managers (Church, 2005).

Herbert Simon (1959) saw intuition as a distilled experience. While furthering the study of executive decision making, he concluded that separating between logical and non-logical mental processes is inaccurate. "Dr. Simon believes that intuition is not a process that operates independently of analysis (Agor, 1989)" In 1978, Simon won the Nobel Prize for his work on decision making and the concept of bounded rationality (Klein, 2004).

Westcott (1968) also saw intuition as distilled experience. He conducted several studies to examine intuition (Church, 2005). Some of his studies were focused on examining intuition as inference and subliminal perception. Westcott (1968) examined his students to see the amount of explicit information they need to make decisions. Those who were able to solve problems with relatively few clues were classified as intuitive thinkers (Fields, 2001).

Maslow (1974) conducted research to understand human behavior and motivation. He believed that creativity of the self actualized person is more connected to intuition than finding correct answers (Church, 2005). Jung (1976) did a great deal of work on personality and psychological types. His work of identifying various psychological types led to the Myers-Briggs Type Indicator (MBTI). The test is used to measure various aspects of personality including intuitive ability (Agor, 1989). The AIM survey used in this dissertation is a significantly modified MBTI.

Intuition and gender

One widely-held view is that successful managers are aggressive, forceful, competitive, self confident, independent and have a high need for control (Hayes et al, 2004). Loden (1985) argued that women have a lower need for control and are more cooperative than men. Green and Cassell (1996) suggest that women are often characterized as relatively submissive, nurturing, warm, kind and selfless. In a study of sex stereotypes and leader behavior; Brenner and Bromer (1981) reported that men are described as being more analytical and logical and women as more intuitive.

Sex differences have been cited as the reason why women are under-represented in management; they lack the qualities for success and cannot perform as effectively as male managers (Hayes et al, 2004). In agreeing with this more compassionate and intuitive gendered- view of women, Clares (1999), referred to intuition as one of the valuable contributions that women bring to management. Studies conducted to investigate the validity of this stereotyping did not produce consistent results.

In a study by Wajcman (1996), successful women managers were found to be in most respects, indistinguishable from men in equivalent positions. Alban-Metcalfe and West (1991) found a remarkable similarity in the way female and male managers perceived themselves at work. Donnell and Hall (1980) found no significant difference between male and female managers in their study of 1,000 matched pairs of female and male managers. However, Eagly and Johnson (1990) found support for the absence and presence of differences in their Meta analysis of studies of gender and leadership style (Hayes et. al., 2004). Pacini and Epstein's (1999) study showed that women perceived themselves as intuitive. They report that women are more likely than men to identify themselves as engaging in experiential processing and to judge themselves as being good at it (Aarnio & Lindeman, 2005).

Taggart et al. (1997) found no gender differences in their study of 495 participants in supervisory and management training programs in four countries. The Personal Style Inventory (Taggart and Valenzi, 1990), a 30-item inventory used to assess six information processing modes classified as either rational or intuitive, was used to measure rational and intuitive style. Responses were based on a six-point rating of frequency anchored by 1 (never) and 6 (always).

Kirton (1989) produced results, using the Kirton Adaption-Innovation Inventory that suggested that men may be more intuitive than women. Agor (1986), in a study of 3,000 managers, found that female managers consistently scored higher on intuition than male managers. Parikh et al. (1994) also found women managers to be more intuitive when they surveyed 1,300 senior managers in nine countries using a measure which included both an objective scale of items which represented the intuition-analysis dichotomy and a subjective self rating scale.

Hayes et al's (2004) study of 1,621 subjects in UK revealed that non-manager females are significantly more analytic than their male counterparts. The study also showed that female managers were more intuitive than non-managing females. However, male managers were found to be similar in their uses of intuition to their non-managing male counterparts. The study found no support for the gendered stereotype believes that female managers are more intuitive than their male counterparts. Study sample comprised three sub-samples of UK managers (364 male and 187 female) and three sub-samples of UK non-managers (747 male and 735 female). The samples were all convenience samples.

In summary, the search for gender differences in information processing style has so far produced mixed results. Self report studies produced results showing that men and women support the existence of gender differences in information processing; however some of the results are actually contradictory. Some studies showed that women see themselves as more intuitive than men while a few self-report and in-depth studies showed men as being more intuitive than women. In making sense of the results, Hayes et al. (2004), suggested that observed pattern "appears to lend support to the utility of the structural (Kanter, 1977) and gendered culture (Green and Cassell, 1996) approaches to understanding behavior in organizations". The fact that female managers showed more intuition than their non-managing counterparts was construed to be their way of adapting to a male dominated environment in which success was determined by conformity to certain modes of conduct.

Wajcman (1996, p. 335) argues that "the social construction of management is one in which managerial competence is intrinsically linked to qualities attaching to men". Unless women behave like men it is unlikely that they will be selected for promotion and those who are promoted will be, in all important respects, indistinguishable from men. Eagly and Johnson

(1990) develop a similar argument and suggest that men and women who occupy the same organizational roles will differ very little because they are selected and select themselves into these roles according to the same set of organizationally relevant criteria, and because organizations usually provide clear guidelines on how incumbents should behave when occupying such roles. "An incidental finding of Eagly and Johnson's (1990) Meta analysis was that the similarity between male and female leadership style is related to the gender ratios in organizations. Female managers are most likely to display masculine traits in those organizations that are dominated by men (Hayes et al., 2004). Gardiner's (1999) comparative study of 60 male and 60 female managers also found that similarities between male and female managers were greatest in male dominated industries.

Country of Operation

Merriam-Webster online dictionary (2007) had four different definitions for a country: an indefinite usually extended expanse of land, the land of a person's birth, residence, or citizenship, a political state or nation or its territory, the people of a state or district, and rural as distinguished from urban areas. Hofstede (1980) defined culture as a kind of collective programming of the mind which distinguished members of one category of people from another. One of the variables studied in this research is the country of operation. Research question four examined the impact of country of operation on reported use of intuition by executives. The literature review on country of operation is hence focused on culture as countries' distinguishing factor.

Culture can be defined as the way of life of a group of people. Damen (1987) also defined culture as "learned and shared human patterns or models for living". These patterns and models pervade all aspects of human social interaction. The use of proverbs to study cultures is a well-known method in Anthropology. Lovell (2001) said "proverbs can be the eyes that provide a window to a culture' s soul." Prahlad (2001) did a study of Jamaican culture through Jamaican Proverbs gathered from Reggae music. In studying Hong Kong and the United States as countries of operation, a review of literatures containing Western and Chinese proverbs was conducted.

The book of Analects is one of the most revered sources of information on Chinese culture. The book contains most of the sayings of Confucius and other highly respected

Chinese teachers. Relevant contents of the book were contrasted with Hofstede's cultural universals to develop a comprehensive outlook on the Chinese culture. The same procedure was carried out for Western culture to develop a comprehensive view of that culture as well.

Hofstede (1980) defined culture as a kind of collective programming of the mind which distinguished members of one category of people from another. In the 1970's, he measured elements of national cultural systems that impact behavior in work situations. His studies produced a total of 116,000 questionnaires in two surveys held in 1968 and 1972 (Hofstede, 2003). The studies revealed four main dimensions on which country cultures differ. They were labeled power distance, uncertainty avoidance, individualism, and masculinity. Later research, which dealt with Asians as the subject, added the dimension called "long-term orientation. These five dimensions were used to compare the two cultures through the eyes of their proverbs.

Power distance index (PDI) focuses on the degree of equality, or inequality, between people in the country's society. A high power distance ranking indicates that inequalities of power and wealth have been allowed to grow within the society. "Hong Kong's power distance score is 68 compared to the other Far East Asian countries average of 60. This is indicative of inequality of power and wealth within the society (Hofstede, 2003). A review of the book of Analects revealed the following Chinese proverbs.

"Yu Tzu said: There are few who have developed themselves filially and fraternally who enjoy offending their superiors. Those who do not enjoy offending superiors are never troublemakers. The Superior Man concerns himself with the fundamentals. Once the fundamentals are established, the proper way (Tao) appears. Are not filial piety and obedience to elders fundamental to the enactment of humaneness?" (Lau, 1992, p. 1) The concept of superiors practiced in China is a reflection of the people's belief in power distance. Confucius in this proverb demonstrates the need to avoid offending those who occupy higher positions in the power structure of the society. Parents are the most prominent superiors in Chinese worldview.

"Meng I Tzu asked about the meaning of filial piety. Confucius said, 'It means 'not diverging (from your parents).' Later, when Fan Chih was driving him, Confucius told Fan Chih, Meng Sun asked me about the meaning of filial piety, and I told him 'not diverging.' Fan Chih said, what did you mean by that? Confucius said, "When your parents are alive, serve them with propriety; when they die, bury them with propriety, and then worship them with propriety." (Lau, 1992, p. 2) The need to serve those who are more powerful than one in Chinese culture is also a proof of the acceptance of power inequality in the society.

"Tzu Lu asked about the meaning of filial piety. Confucius said, Nowadays filial piety means being able to feed your parents. But everyone does this for even horses and dogs. Without respect, what's the difference? (Lau, 1992, p. 2) Dictionary.com defined respect as deference to a privileged position. Confucius here again affirms the acceptance of power inequality in Chinese culture by asking for deference from those who are less powerful in the society.

"Tzu Hsia asked about filial piety. Confucius said, what is important is the expression you show in your face. You should not understand 'filial' to mean merely the young doing physical tasks for their parents, or giving them food and wine when it is available." (Lau, 1992, p. 2) Confucius here demonstrates the need to even make provisions available to those who are more powerful to one in the society. It is another affirmation of the acceptance of power inequality in the society.

Individualism (IDV) focuses on the extent to which the society reinforces individual or collective achievement and interpersonal relationships (Hofstede, 2003). A high individualism ranking indicates that individuality and individual rights are paramount within the society. Individuals in these societies may tend to form a larger number of looser relationships. A low individualism ranking typifies societies of a more collectivist nature with close ties between individuals. Hong Kong ranked low on individualism with a score of 25, second highest for Far East Asian countries, behind Japan's 46 ranking, and compared to an average of 24 for Asian countries. Corresponding quotes from the book of Analects are stated as follows:

"Tzu Kung asked, 'Does the Superior Man also have things that he hates?' Confucius said; He does. He hates those who advertise the faults of others. He hates those who abide in lowliness and slander the great. He hates those who are bold without propriety. He hates those who are convinced of their own perfection, and closed off to anything else. How about you, what do you hate? Tzu Kung said I hate those who take a little bit of clarity as wisdom; I hate those who take disobedience as courage; I hate those who take disclosing people's weak points to be straightforwardness." (Lau, 1992, p.17) Confucius here demonstrates the need to avoid exposing others weaknesses. The need to outdo others is almost non-existing in Chinese worldview. This is in sharp contrast to Western worldview of self before others.

"Confucius said: When you serve your mother and father it is okay to try to correct them once in a while. But if you see that they are not going to listen to you, keep your respect for them and don't distance yourself from them. Work without complaining." (Lau, 1992, p. 4) Here Confucius emphasizes the need to conform and to try to blend into the society. He said even if your parents would not take your advice, you still need to be part of the group they belong to.

"The Duke of Sheh told Confucius: In my land, there are Just men. If a father steals a sheep, the son will testify against him. Confucius said, "The Just men in my land are different from this. The father conceals the wrongs of his son, and the son conceals the wrongs of his father. This is Rightness!" (Lau, 1992, p. 13) Confucius affirms the need to conceal rather than expose the shortcomings of members of one's group.

Masculinity (MAS) focuses on the extent to which a society reinforces, or does not reinforce, the traditional masculine work role model of male achievement, control, and power (Hofstede, 2003). A high masculinity ranking indicates the country experiences a high degree of gender differentiation. In these cultures, males dominate a significant portion of the society and power structure, with females being controlled by male domination.

A low masculinity ranking indicates the country has a low level of differentiation and discrimination between genders. In these cultures, females are treated equally to males in all aspects of the society. Quotes relevant to masculinity in the book of Analects are stated as follows:

"Being robbed, Chi K'ang Tzu was upset, and questioned Confucius about what to do. Confucius said, "If you were desire less, they wouldn't steal from you, even if you were to offer them a reward to do so." (Lau, 1992, p. 12) The authentic original Chinese culture does not favor materialism. In fact, the society esteems peace and harmony above competitiveness. Confucius here seems to convey the need to shun materialism.

"A shih who is set on the way, but is ashamed of old clothes and coarse food, is not worth consulting." (Lau, 1992, p. 4) Tao is often regarded as the way and the Chinese culture's aim is to develop the superior man who is not bothered about material possessions. In this teaching Confucius is emphasizing again the need to develop the moral self and not necessarily material possessions.

"Confucius said: A worthy becomes free of the world, then he becomes free of his land; then he becomes free from lust; then he becomes free from language." (Lau, 1992, p. 14) The masculine male role model of male achievement is again de-emphasized in this teaching as Confucius encourages freedom from the desire for material possession.

"Duke Ching of Ch'i had a thousand teams of horses, but when he died, there was nothing for which the people could praise him. Po Yi and Shu Ch'i died of starvation at the foot of Shou Yang Mountain, and the people praise them up till this day. What meaning can you glean from this?" (Lau, 1992, p. 16) Confucius here seems to be saying that a person's legacy is more than material possessions left behind. A superior man is in essence not the one who left a lot of material possessions for his descendants, but the one who left a good name for his descendants by way of living a morally superior life.

Uncertainty avoidance index (UAI) focuses on the level of tolerance for uncertainty and ambiguity within the society - i.e. unstructured situations (Hofstede, 2003). A high uncertainty avoidance ranking indicates the country has a low tolerance for uncertainty and ambiguity. This creates a rule-oriented society that institutes laws, rules, regulations, and controls in order to reduce the amount of uncertainty. A low uncertainty avoidance ranking indicates the country has less concern about ambiguity and uncertainty and has more tolerance for a variety of opinions. This is reflected in a society that is less rule-oriented, more readily accepts change, and takes more and greater risks.

Hong Kong is relatively low in uncertainty avoidance. The country's (UAI) is only 29, compared to an average of 63 for the Far East Asian countries. This very low level of uncertainty avoidance is the fourth lowest in the World, with only Denmark (23), Jamaica (13), and Singapore (8) having lower scores for this dimension. A search through the book of Analects revealed the following sayings about the dimension:

Chi Lu asked about serving the spirits. Confucius said, "If you can't yet serve men, how can you serve the spirits?" Lu said, "May I ask about death?" Confucius said, "If you don't understand what life is, how will you understand death?" (Lau, 1992, p. 11) Confucius in this teaching shows how Chinese people are generally intolerant of ambiguity. The emphasis in this teaching is to focus on what you know and leave the ambiguous for other people.

Tzu Kung asked who was the most worthy between Shih and Shang. The Master said, "Shih goes too far, Shang does not go far enough." "Then is Shih superior?" The Master said, "Going too far is the same as not going far enough." (Lau, 1992, p. 11) The need for precision is emphasized in this teaching by Confucius. He said someone did not go far enough and the other one went too far. This is an affirmation of Chinese societies' high score on this dimension. Hong Kong's relatively low score on this dimension might be a reflection of British's influence on the former colony.

Long-term orientation (LTO) focuses on the extent to which the society embraces, or does not embrace long-term devotion to traditional, forward thinking values. High long-term orientation ranking indicates the country subscribe to the values of long-term commitments and respect for tradition. This is thought to support a strong work ethic where long-term rewards are expected as a result of today's hard work. A low long-term orientation ranking indicates the country does not reinforce the concept of long-term, traditional orientation. In this culture, change can occur more rapidly as long-term traditions and commitments do not become impediments to change.

"Hong Kong's Geert Hofstede analysis has long-term orientation (LTO) as the highest-ranking (96) factor, which is true for all Far East Asian cultures. This dimension indicates a societies' time perspective and an attitude of persevering; that is, overcoming obstacles with time, if not with will and strength" (Hofstede, 2003). LTO related quotes from the book of Analects are stated below:

"Confucius said: The superior man stands in awe of three things: He is in awe of the decree of Heaven; He is in awe of great men; He is in awe of the words of the sages. The inferior man does not know the decree of Heaven; he takes great men lightly, and laughs at the words of the sages" (Lau, 1992, p. 16) Respect for tradition is implied by the reference to great men in this teaching. Hong Kong scored very high in this index indicating that respect for tradition is still important in the enclave.

"The men of Lu were rebuilding the Main Treasury. Min Tzu Ch'ien said: Why don't we keep its old style? Why do we have to change it completely?" Confucius said, this fellow doesn't say much, but when he does, he is right on the mark." (Lau, 1992, p. 11) The reference to keeping the old style in this teaching is an affirmation of the Chinese culture's respect for tradition. It is an affirmation of the enclave's high score on the LTO index.

"Fan Chih wanted to ask about agriculture. Confucius said, why don't you ask an old farmer? Fan Chih then said that he would like to learn about gardening. Confucius said, why don't you ask an old gardener? Fan Chih left. Confucius said, Fan is really simple, isn't he? If the men in charge love propriety, the people cannot stand to be disrespectful. If the men in charge love rightness, then the people cannot stand not to follow them. If the men in charge love trust, then the people cannot stand not to respond with their emotions. If you were to govern in this way, the people would come flocking to your kingdom, carrying their babies on their backs. Why do you have to worry about agriculture?" (Lau, 1992, p. 13) Referring to old Gardner and old farmer in this teaching is a way of showing respect for tradition. Confucius again affirms Hong Kong's high LTO score in Hofstede's dimensions.

Only seven (7) countries in the Geert Hofstede research have individualism (IDV) as their highest dimension: USA (91), Australia (90), United Kingdom (89), Netherlands and Canada (80), and Italy (76). The high individualism (IDV) ranking for the United States indicates a society with a more individualistic attitude and relatively loose bonds with others. The populace is more self-reliant and individuals look out for themselves and their close family members. Review of

Western proverb literatures produced two groups of proverbs relating to individualism. The first group promotes individualism while the second group promotes cooperation. The two groups are presented below.

Every man must carry his own cross

If you want a thing done right, do it yourself

If you want breakfast in bed, sleep in the kitchen

Paddle your own canoe

Good fences make good neighbors

You are responsible for you

The need for individuals to fetch for themselves is expressed in these proverbs. The central theme of the six proverbs is that individuals should be prepared to solve their problems without relying on others for help. This is in line with the USA's high score of 91 on this cultural dimension. However, the literature review also revealed some proverbs that promote cooperation more than individualism. Examples of proverbs in this category are presented below.

A bicycle can't stand on its own because it's two-tired.

Honey catches more flies than vinegar.

No man is an island

The nail that sticks out gets pounded

A big tree attracts the woodsman's axe

The central theme of these five proverbs seems to be at odds with the earlier six. They encourage cooperation rather than individualism. The possibility of some of the proverbs being foreign is also real since the American society is not entirely white. The most unusual of the proverbs is fourth one that talks about nails getting pounded. The researcher felt this particular proverb might have been imported from Asia.

The next highest Hofstede dimension for the United States is masculinity (MAS) with a ranking of 62, compared with an average of 50 for all countries. This indicates the country experiences a higher degree of gender differentiation of roles. The male dominates a significant portion of the society and power structure. This situation generates a female population that becomes more assertive and competitive, with women shifting toward the male role model and away from their female role.

The literature review for this section turned up proverbs that mostly support USA's score on the dimension. The supporting proverbs are presented before those that are not supportive of the position.

Half a loaf is better than none.

If at first you don't succeed, try, try again.

It's the early bird that gets the worm.

Make hay while the sun shines.

The need to keep trying until success is achieved is expressed in the second proverb, this is indicative of the male achievement model valued by the culture. The essence of timeliness in trying to achieve the desired societal status is emphasized by the third proverb. Two proverbs that are not supportive of the male dominant, achievement oriented tendency are listed below. The two proverbs look more like what one would find in Asian cultural literatures.

Winning isn't everything.

Health is better than wealth.

The United States was included in the group of countries that had the long term orientation (LTO) dimension added. The LTO is the lowest dimension for the US at 29, compared with an average of 45 for all countries. This low LTO ranking is indicative of the societies' belief in meeting its obligations. The first group of proverbs gathered from the literature review supports the low score of the country on the dimension, while the second group seems to suggest that the score on the dimension should have been higher. The supporting proverbs are presented hereby presented.

Never put off till (until) tomorrow what you can do today.

No time like the present.

A stitch in time saves nine

The second proverb in this second group is actually more favorable towards long term orientation as people are encouraged to make attempts to understand the past in dealing with the future. The third is also similar in its theme as people are encouraged to focus more on the long run.

All things come to him who waits.

He who fails to study the past is doomed to repeat it.

History repeats itself.

Nature, time, and patience are three great physicians.

The next lowest ranking Dimension for the United States is power distance (PDI) at 40, compared to an average of 55 for all nations. This is indicative of a greater equality between societal levels, including government, organizations, and even within families. This orientation reinforces a cooperative interaction across power levels and creates a more stable cultural environment.

A cat may look at a king.

Green leaves and brown leaves fall from the same tree.

If you want to judge a man's character, give him power.

Power corrupts; absolute power corrupts absolutely.

The society's disdain for power permeates through the four proverbs. This is also reflected in the country's very low PDI score. Egalitarianism is one of the central tenets of the American society. The first proverb relates human freedom to look to that of a cat. "If a cat may look at the king - then I have a right to look where I please" Egalitarianism is also further stressed by the fact that we all emanate from the same source as expressed in the green leaf proverb. The proverb implies that we are all the same inside regardless of what we look like outside.

The last Geert Hofstede Dimension for the US is uncertainty avoidance (UAI), with a ranking of 46, compared to an average of 64 for all countries. A low ranking in the uncertainty avoidance dimension is indicative of a society that has fewer rules and does not attempt to control all outcomes and results. It also has a greater level of tolerance for a variety of ideas, thoughts, and beliefs. Researcher's review of Western proverb literatures produced two groups of proverbs relating to uncertainty. The first group promotes risk taking while the second group promotes the need to exercise caution. The two groups are presented below.

It's easier to ask forgiveness than permission.

It is better to die on one's feet than live on one's knees.

He who hesitates is lost.

He who dares wins

Don't cross a bridge before you come to it.

A watched pot never boils.

A coward dies a thousand times before his death.

The valiant never taste of death but once.

This first group of proverbs encourage risk taking. The fifth proverb claims fretting about future problems is superfluous and the seventh proverb decries cowardice. It teaches that worrying about a forthcoming disaster may cause as much (or even more) pain as the disaster when it occurs (but does neither change it nor make it easier). The central theme of this group of proverbs is that fretting is more destructive than risk taking. This position is affirmed by the country's low UAI score.

The second group promotes cautious approach to risk taking and the proverbs in this group are presented below.

A bird in the hand is worth two in the bush.

A picture is worth a thousand words.

Cobbler, stick to thy last.

Don't burn your bridges before they're crossed.

Don't count your chickens before they're hatched.

It's better to be safe than sorry.

The first proverb in this second group asserts that what you already have is worth more than what you dream about and the third proverb tries to encourage people to stick to what they know. The fourth proverb suggests that people should not act in ways that would leave them with no alternatives. The mitigating effect of this second group of proverbs might be responsible for the middle of the road ranking given to USA on the index.

Intuition, Gender, Country of Operation and Decision Making

Existing literature seem to support the existence of a positive relationship between decision making effectiveness and intuitive skills. Managers who use intuition are more likely to be promoted to senior management positions than those who did not. A study of 2,000 managers by Weston Agor in 1986 showed that top executives rated significantly higher in intuition than middle or low level managers (Agor, 1991). Geert Hofstede's (1973) studies showed that ethnic background does affect employee's attitude towards certain theoretical dimensions. The theoretical dimensions were later called cultural universals. These cultural universals were found to significantly influence managerial effectiveness across cultures.

The link between ethnic background and intuitive decision making has been elusive to establish. Familoni (2003) found no statistical significance in mean differences between the use of intuition by leaders from Nigerian and those from the United States. However, Atsunyo (1992) found that leaders from Ghana tend to rely more heavily on intuition than their United States counterparts. Another study by Agor (1986) showed managers from Asian ethnic backgrounds to be higher in intuitive skills than other managers who participated in the study.

A field study conducted by Agor (1986) showed that top managers use more intuition than low level managers. Agor' s study (1986) also showed statistically significant difference between the use of intuition by male and female managers. Female managers scored higher on the use of intuition than male managers.

Downey (2006) reported another study of 176 female senior managers by Swinburne University's Center for Neuropsychology. The study showed that more successful female managers had more intuitive decision-making skills than their counterparts. Isenberg (1984) found that senior managers relied heavily on intuition. His study showed that 80% of male managers with 10 to 30 years management experience preferred using intuition. Agor (1986) also found that government leaders at national level use more intuition than government leaders at the local level.

Studies conducted by Agor (1986) also showed that Personnel managers tend to be more intuitive in their decision making than Financial Managers and Military leaders. Studies showed that managers tend to deny their uses of intuition in decision making. "Positional leaders who use the traditional decision-making approaches may deny and/or suppress the value of using intuition in decision making and may not acknowledge the value of intuition as a source of power in the workplace (Church, 2005)"

Conclusion

The concept of using intuition in managerial decision making is still not as popular as one would expect. Business students are essentially exposed to left brain management decision making techniques despite the preponderance of evidence showing that managers who make it to senior executive levels are intuitive (right brained) in their decision making. The next few chapters report findings of a comparative study conducted by the author to examine usage of right side of the brain by managers in two countries; United States and Hong Kong.

Research Design

The need for full brain managerial decision making cannot be adequately articulated without a proper study of the current state of managerial decision making. Since left brain rational decision making is the established norm, the impetus is on understanding the state of right brain managerial decision making. In order to further understand the status of this less studied aspect of managerial decision making, a comparative study of right brain intuitive decision making was conducted by this researcher and the findings of the study are presented below. The study was developed to test the validity of the current assertion that strong relationships exist among a manager's gender, management level, management's experience, country of operation, and their reported uses of intuition in decision making

(Atsunyo, 1992; Agor, 1986; Downey, 2006; Isenberg, 1984).

Research designs can be experimental, quasi-experimental or non-experimental. This research design is non-experimental since the goal of the study was to examine the relationship between dependent and independent variables in a non cause-effect asserting way. Non-experimental research designs are often referred to as correlational. A study qualifies as correlational if the data lend themselves only to interpretations about the degree to which certain things tend to co-occur or are related to each other (Price, 2000) The research design is, therefore, correlational in nature.

The variables of this study consisted of five independent variables and one dependent variable as listed below.

Independent Variables: Gender, Management Level, Management Experience, and Country of Operation

Dependent Variable: Reported use of intuition in decision making.

Further, the study employed a quantitative approach to seek empirical support for the hypotheses developed from theories of intuitive decision making. The quantitative data that was gathered using Agor's Intuitive Measurement Survey questionnaires was used to ensure an accurate empirical analysis without bias. The questionnaire instrument examined relationships among the variables including independent and dependent variables.

The research tested statistical hypotheses. Most responses by Hong Kong and US managers and supervisors were quantified along 5-point scales, or as interval variables classified into one of two, three, four, or five alternative classes. Ratio and nominal variables were also included in this research.

Data Sources

Data sources were private and public organizations in Hong Kong and the United States. The research populations were defined as leaders, supervisors and managers of Hong Kong and United States private and public organizations. The sample population for research in the United States was selected from a representative set of U.S. firms. In Hong Kong, the sample population was also selected from a representative set of Hong Kong firms. Subjects of the study were 200 leaders/managers selected from these organizations. Agor's Intuitive Measurement (AIM) was used to test for leaders reported use of intuition in decision making.

Purposeful, criterion, maximum variation, and convenience sampling techniques were used to select the 200 leaders, supervisors, and managers interviewed for this study. Purposeful sampling selects information rich cases for in-depth study. In criteria-based sampling the researcher selects a criterion and picks all cases that meet that criterion. Convenience sampling involves selecting handy elementary units from a population for observation. Maximum variation sampling involves purposefully picking a wide range of variation on dimensions of interest (Mugo, 2007).

The qualifying criteria for participation were: (a) participants must be or have been in a leadership position (b) and be a resident of either Hong Kong or the United States. The selected criteria and qualifying questions assisted in ensuring the appropriateness of the participants. Online company directories, hard copy company directories, and other equally current sources were used to locate participants for the survey.

To obtain the quantitative data, questionnaires were sent via electronic mailing system to selected companies with a cover letter. To increase the rate of return, the cover letter also requested recipients to forward the questionnaire to their colleagues who met the study' s criteria (see Appendices A & B).

Each participant was electronically sent a link that led to a web page containing the survey questions. Once the respondent clicks submit, the questionnaire was mailed directly to the researcher. Further, usable data refers to questionnaire responses with incomplete answers.

Population and Sample

The sample population for research in the United States was selected from a representative set of U.S. firms. In Hong Kong, the sample population was also selected from a representative set of Hong Kong firms. Subjects of the study were 200 leaders/managers selected from these organizations. Agor's Intuitive Measurement (AIM) was used to test for leaders reported use of intuition in decision making.

Procedures and Measures

The quantitative research employed Agor's Intuitive Measurement Survey (with permission by copyright owner). The AIM survey was administered to 100 participants from the US and 100 participants from Hong Kong. Questions on the survey were developed to measure all independent and dependent variables.

Questions on the survey measured the following variables: Gender, Management Level, Management Experience, Country of Operation, and Reported use of intuition in decision making.

Validity and Reliability of the Instrument

AIM Survey (Agor's Intuitive Measurement Survey) is a modified MBTI (Myers-Briggs Type Indicator). The instrument, therefore, uses the reliability and validity of MBTI (Agor, 1984). Studies have found strong support for construct validity, internal consistency, and test related reliability of MBTI instrument (Thompson & Borello, 1986). Further, the instrument was designed to best measure all the variables in this study. The questionnaire was modified and simplified so it contained clear instructions, questions, and possible answers.

Independent Variables

The four independent variables are Gender, Management Level, Management Experience, and Country of Operation. The variables were measured by questions on the questionnaire, and relationships between each variable and question are described as follows.

Gender

Respondents were asked to indicate their gender by choosing between male and female in question 17 of the survey.

Management level

Three management level choices were specified in the survey. In question 18 respondents were asked to choose between supervisor, manager and executive management levels. Questions 13, 14, and 15 also reinforced the measure.

Management experience

Management experience was measured by the number of years respondents spent in management positions. In question 16 respondents were asked to state the number of years they have worked as supervisor or manager.

Country of operation

The study also examined the difference between the reported use of intuition in managerial decision making between managers residing in Hong Kong and those residing in the United States. In obtaining data for this measure, respondents were asked to indicate their country of residence by choosing between Hong Kong and the United States in question 20.

Dependent Variable

This study has one dependent variable which is reported use of intuition in decision making. This variable was measured by 12 questions on the questionnaire.

Reported use of intuition in decision making

This variable was evaluated by the respondent's response to questions 1 through 12 on the survey. All A responses on questions 1,3,5,6 and 11 received a score of 1 each and B responses on questions 2,4,7,8,9,10 and 12 also received 1 point each. The total of the "a" and "b" scores is the respondent's intuitive score. To obtain the thinking score from the intuitive score, the intuitive score is subtracted from 12.

Questions 13, 14, and 15 were used to ensure respondents actually qualify for the study. Responses with no on all three questions were set aside.

Null Hypotheses

Hypothesis 1: There is no relationship between a US manager's reported use of intuition in decision making and the manager's management level, measured at the .05 level of significance.

Hypothesis 2: There is no relationship between a Hong Kong manager's reported use of intuition in decision making and the manager's management level, measured at the .05 level of significance.

Hypothesis 3: There is no relationship between a US manager's reported use of intuition in decision making and the manager's level of management experience, measured at the .05 level of significance.

Hypothesis 4: There is no relationship between Hong Kong manager's reported use of intuition in decision making and the manager's level of management experience, measured at the .05 level of significance.

Hypothesis 5: US female managers' reported use of intuition in decision making is not significantly different from US male managers' reported use of intuition in decision making, measured at the .05 level of significance.

Hypothesis 6: Hong Kong female managers' reported use of intuition in decision making is not different from Hong Kong male managers' reported use of intuition in decision making, measured at the .05 level of significance.

Hypothesis 7: Managers operating in Hong Kong are not significantly different in their reported uses of intuition in decision making from managers operating in the US, measured at the .05 level of significance.

Alternative Hypotheses

Hypothesis 1: There is a positive relationship between a US manager's reported use of intuition in decision making and the manager's management level, measured at the .05 level of significance.

Hypothesis 2: There is a positive relationship between a Hong Kong manager's reported use of intuition in decision making and the manager's management level, measured at the .05 level of significance.

Hypothesis 3: There is a positive relationship between a US manager's reported use of intuition in decision making and the manager's level of management experience, measured at the .05 level of significance.

Hypothesis 4: There is a positive relationship between Hong Kong manager's reported use of intuition in decision making and the manager's level of management experience, measured at the .05 level of significance.

Hypothesis 5: US female managers' reported use of intuition in decision making is higher than US male managers' reported use of intuition in decision making, measured at the .05 level of significance.

Hypothesis 6: Hong Kong female managers' reported use of intuition in decision making is higher than Hong Kong male managers' reported use of intuition in decision making, measured at the .05 level of significance.

Hypothesis 7: Managers operating in Hong Kong are higher in their reported uses of intuition in decision making than managers operating in the US, measured at the .05 level of significance.

Level of Significance

The study's hypotheses were individually tested at the 0.05 level of significance. In generalizing from the results of a sample to the population it represents, it is needful to determine the level of error the researcher is willing to tolerate (Connor-Linton, 2003). A five percent chance of being wrong in generalizing from the data to the population is deemed appropriate in cases where the stakes are not extremely high. The consequence of being wrong in this case is considered to be quite minimal as in similar studies where the .05 level of significance has been deemed appropriate in the past. A .05 level of significance is, therefore, set for the various hypotheses of this study. A corollary of this choice is that a 5 percent chance of incorrectly rejecting the hypothesis that no significant relationship subsist between the reported use of intuition by managers and their genders does exist.

MANAGEMENT LEVEL AND BRAIN USAGE

Research Question 1: What is the relationship between management level and reported use of intuition in decision making?

Finding 1.1: Hong Kong's business owners with 10 years or less' use of intuition is lower than US supervisors with 10 years or less. Mean scores of Hong Kong Business owners 6.0; US supervisors 6.35. Significance is at the .022 level.

This finding show that Hong Kong senior level executives who participated in the study used less intuitive right brain decision making skills than low level United States supervisors who participated in the study. This difference is presented in Table 1 below.

Table 1

The Difference between Reported use of Intuition score of Hong Kong Business owners with 10 years or less management experience and US supervisors with 10 years or less management experience.

Variable	N	Minimum	Maximum	Mean	Std. Deviation
SCUS	20	2	10	6.35	2.1830
SCHK6	9	3	11	6	2.5

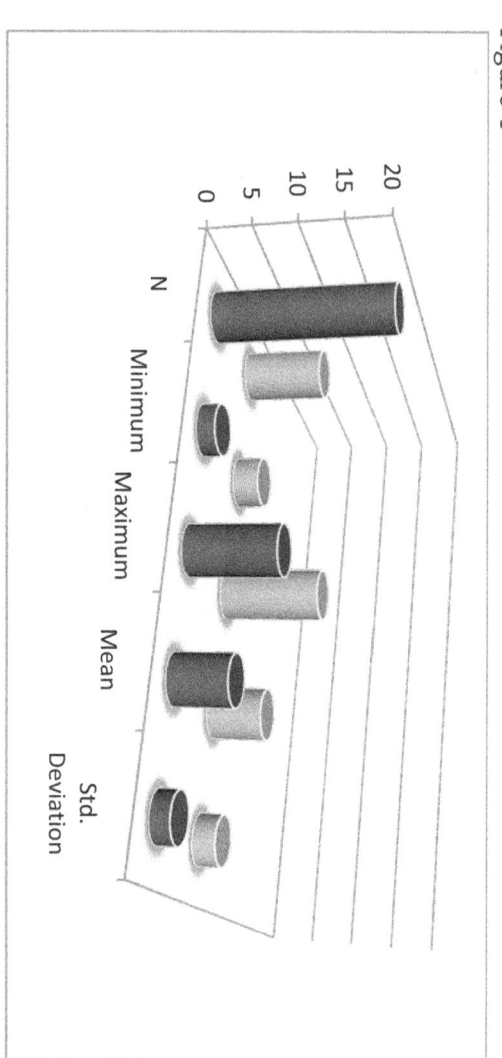

Figure 1

Finding 1.2: US managers with 10 years or less use of intuition is lower than US supervisors with over 10 years. Mean scores of US managers with 10 years or less is 7.1304; US supervisors with over 10 years is 8.00. Significance is at the 0.01 level.

This finding show that fairly experienced US managers who participated in the study used less intuitive right brain decision making skills than more experienced US supervisors who participated in the study. This difference is presented in Table 2 below.

Table 2

The Difference between Reported use of Intuition score of US managers with 10 years or less management experience and US supervisors with over 10 years management experience.

Variable	N	Minimum	Maximum	Mean	Std. Deviation
SCUS2	23	1	12	7.1304	2.5281
SCUS1	2	7	9	8	1.4142

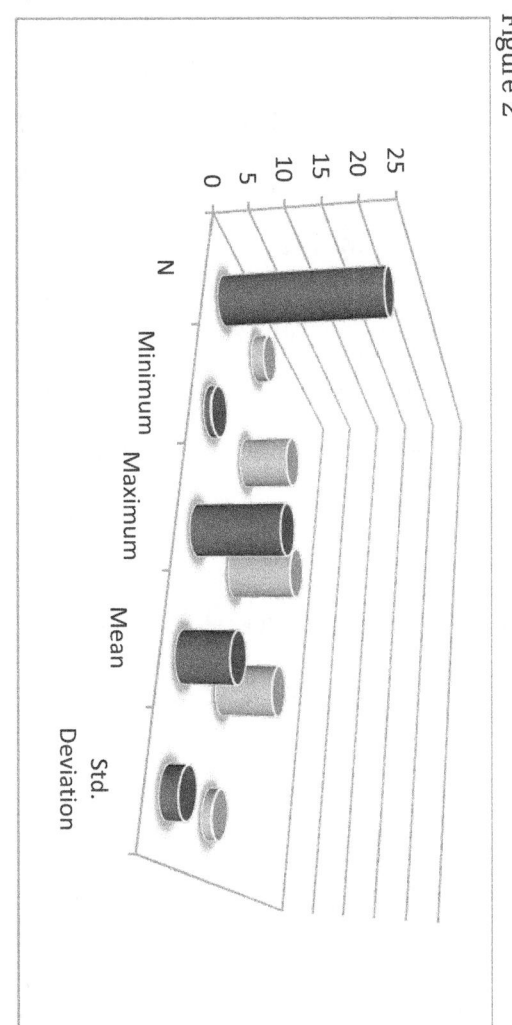

Figure 2

Finding 1.3: US managers with more than 10 years' use of intuition is higher than US supervisors with over 10 years use. Mean scores of US managers with more than 10 years is 8.5714; US supervisors with over 10 years is 8.00. Significant is at the 0.01 level.

This finding show that highly experienced United States managers who participated in the study used more intuitive right brain decision making skills than equally experienced United States supervisors who participated in the study. This difference is presented in Table 3 and Figure 3 below.

Table 3

The Difference between Reported use of Intuition score of US managers with more than 10 years management experience and US supervisors with over 10 years management experience.

Variable	N	Minimum	Maximum	Mean	Std. Deviation
SCUS3	7	7	11	8.5714	1.7182
SCUS1	2	7	9	8	1.4142

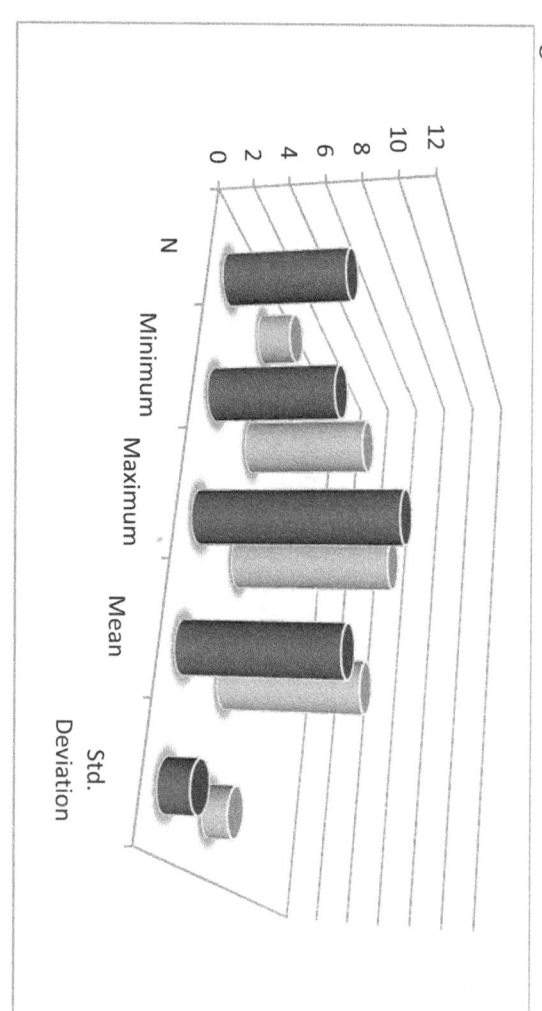

Figure 3

Finding 1.4: US executives with 10 years or less' use of intuition in decision making is lower than US supervisors with over 10 years. Mean scores of US executives with 10 years or less is 6.666; US supervisors with over 10 years is 8.00. This result is significant at the 0.01 level.

This finding show that fairly experienced US executives who participated in the study used less intuitive right brain decision making skills than more experienced US supervisors who participated in the study. This difference is presented in Table 4 below.

Table 4

The Difference between Reported use of Intuition score of US executives with 10 years or less management experience and US supervisors with over 10 years management experience.

Variable	N	Minimum	Maximum	Mean	Std. Deviation
SCUS4	9	4	9	6.6666	1.93649
SCUS1	2	7	9	8	1.4142

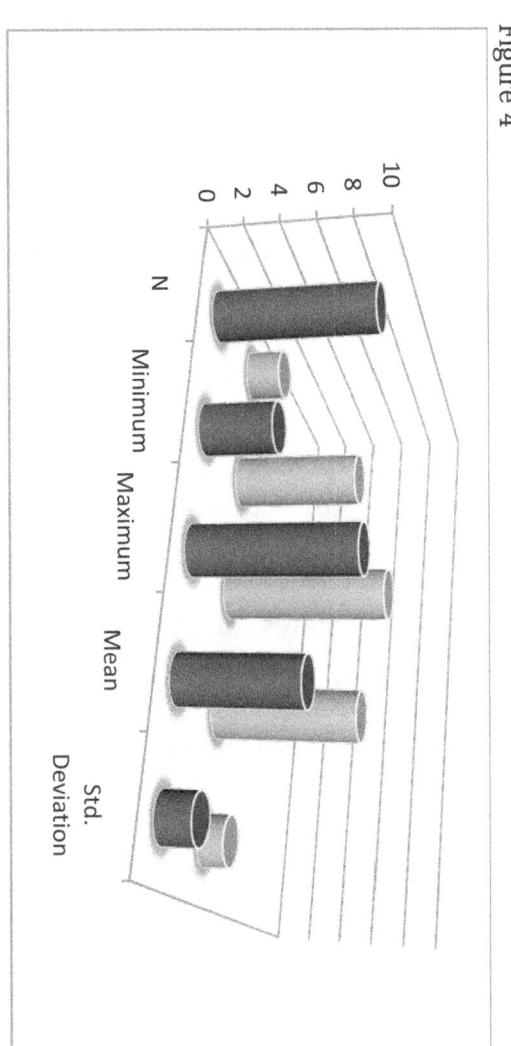

Figure 4

Finding 1.5: US executives with over 10 years' use of intuition in decision making is lower than US supervisors with over 10 years. Mean scores of US executives with over 10 years is 7.6666; US supervisors with over 10 years is 8.00. Significance is at the 0.01 level.

This finding show that highly experienced United States executives who participated in the study used less intuitive right brain decision making skills than equally experienced United States supervisors who participated in the study. This difference is presented in Table 5 and Figure 5 below.

Table 5

The Difference between Reported use of Intuition score of US executives with over 10 years management experience and US supervisors with over 10 years management experience.

Variable	N	Minimum	Maximum	Mean	Std. Deviation
SCUS5	18	4	11	7.6666	1.940285
SCUS1	2	7	9	8	1.4142

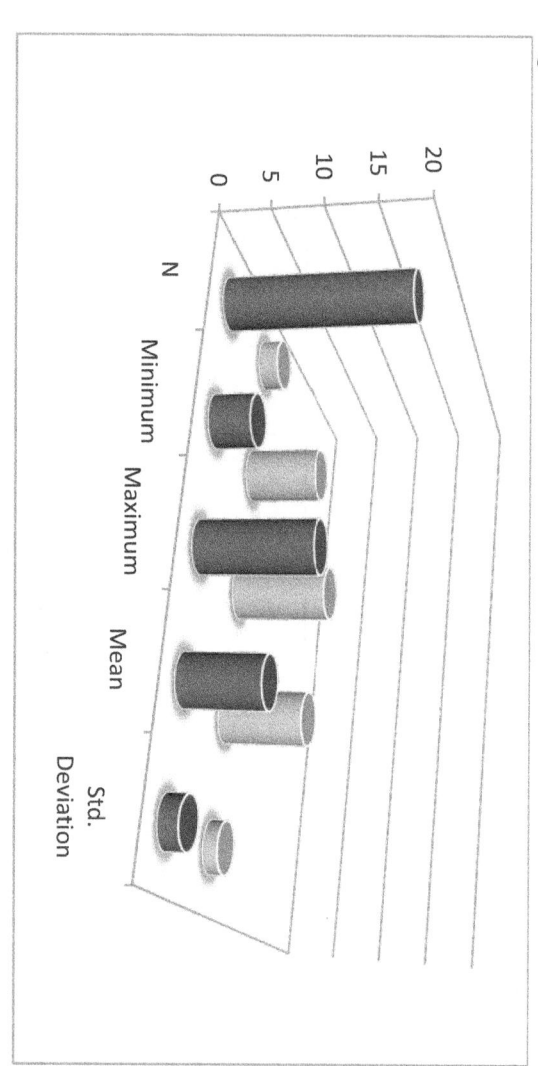

Figure 5

Finding 1.6: US business owners with over 10 years' use of intuition in decision making is lower than US supervisors with over 10 years. Mean scores of US business owners with over 10 years is 6.18181; US supervisors with over 10 years is 8.00. Significance is at the 0.01 level.

This finding show that highly experienced United States business owners who participated in the study used less intuitive right brain decision making skills than equally experienced United States supervisors who participated in the study. This difference is presented in Table 6 and Figure 6 below.

Table 6

The Difference between Reported use of Intuition score of US business owners with over 10 years management experience and US supervisors with over 10 years management experience.

Variable	N	Minimum	Maximum	Mean	Std. Deviation
SCUS7	11	3	11	6.18181	2.67649
SCUS1	2	7	9	8	1.4142

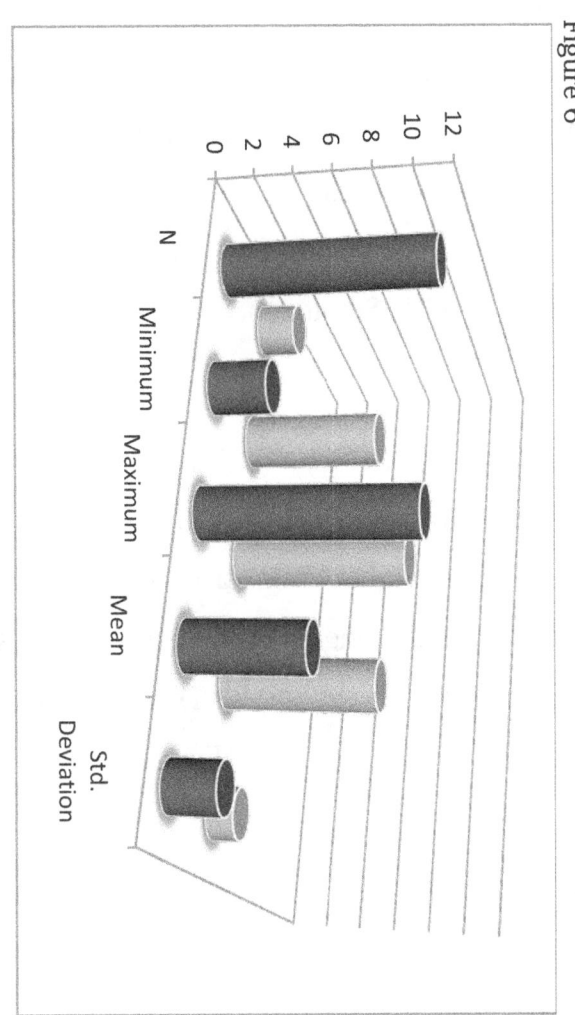

Figure 6

Finding 1.7: Hong Kong male executives' use of intuition in decision making is higher than Hong Kong male business owners' use of intuition in decision making. Mean scores of Hong Kong male executives is 7.933; Hong Kong male business owners is 6.583. Significance is at the .022 level.

This finding show that Hong Kong male executives who participated in the study used more intuitive right brain decision making skills than Hong Kong male business owners who participated in the study. This difference is presented in Table 7 and Figure 7 below.

Table 7

The Difference between Reported use of Intuition score of Hong Kong male executives *and* Hong Kong male business owners.

Variable	N	Minimum	Maximum	Mean	Std. Deviation
SCHK6	15	4	11	7.93333	1.9808
SCHK7	12	4	11	6.5833	2.2343

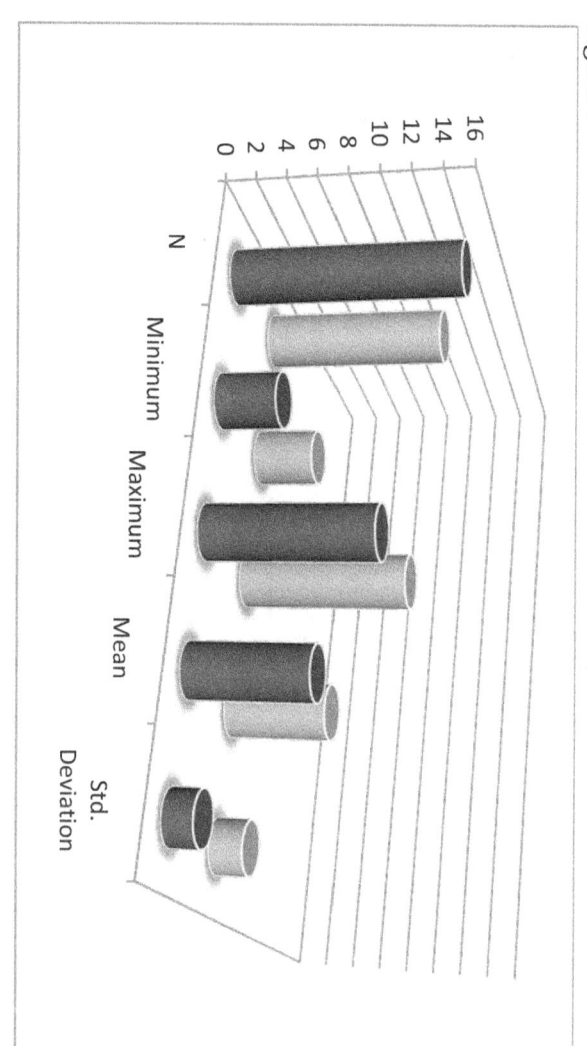

Figure 7

EXPERIENCE AND BRAIN USAGE

Research Question 2: What is the relationship between work experience and use of intuition in decision making?

Finding 2.1: US supervisors with 10 years or less' use of intuition in decision making is lower than US supervisors with over 10 years. Mean scores of US supervisors with 10 years or less is 6.35; US supervisors with over 10 years is 8.00. Significance is at the 0.01 level.

This finding show that fairly experienced US supervisors who participated in the study used less intuitive right brain decision making skills than more experienced US supervisors who participated in the study. This difference is presented in Table 8 below.

Table 8

The Difference between Reported use of Intuition score of US supervisors with 10 years or less management experience and US supervisors with over 10 years management experience.

Variable	N	Minimum	Maximum	Mean	Std. Deviation
SCUS	20	2	10	6.35	2.1830
SCUS1	2	7	9	8	1.4142

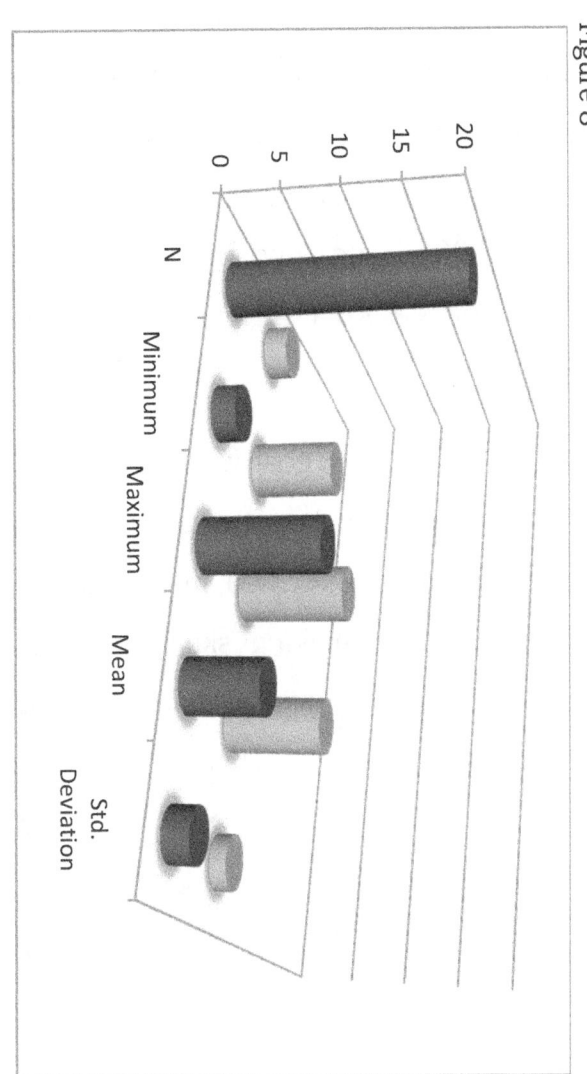

Figure 8

Finding 2.2: US female managers with more than 20 years' use of intuition in decision making is higher than Hong Kong female managers with 5 years or less. Mean scores of US female managers with more than 20 years is 7.666 Hong Kong female managers with 5 years or less is 7.1. Significance is at the .020 level.

This finding show that well experienced United States female managers who participated in the study used more intuitive right brain decision making skills than less experienced Hong Kong female managers who participated in the study. This difference is presented in Table 9 and Figure 9 below.

Table 9

The Difference between Reported use of Intuition score of US female managers with more than 20 years management experience and Hong Kong female managers with 5 years or less management experience.

Variable	N	Minimum	Maximum	Mean	Std. Deviation
SCUS3	6	3	10	7.666666667	2.503331114
SCHK	20	3	11	7.1	2.468752082

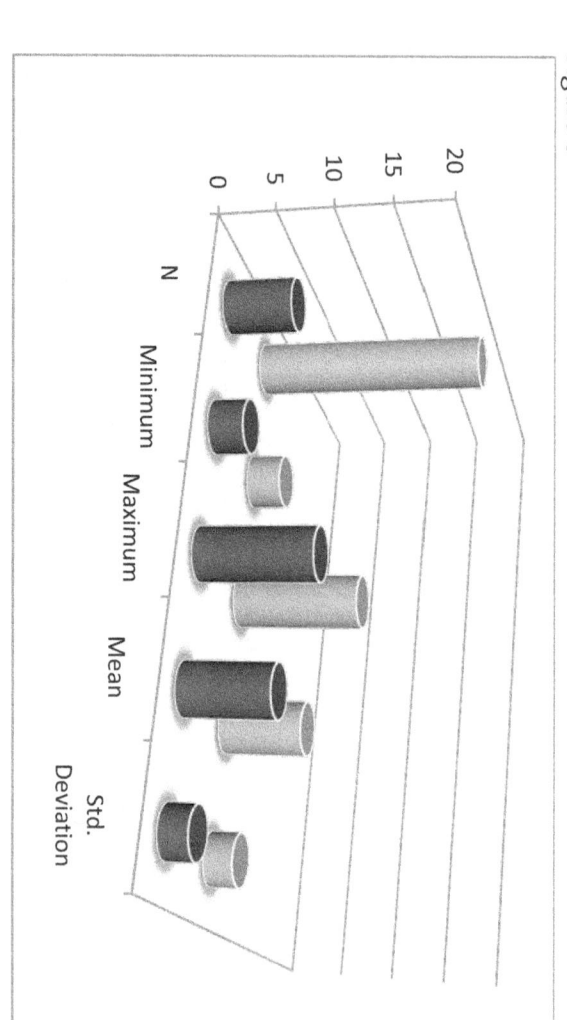

Figure 9

Finding 2.3: US male managers with between 6 and 10 years use of intuition in decision making is lower than US male managers with 5 years or less . Mean scores of US male managers with between 6 and 10 years is 7.00; US male managers with 5 years or less is 9.5. Significance is at the .010 level.

This finding show that moderately experienced United States male managers who participated in the study used less intuitive right brain decision making skills than less experienced United States male managers who participated in the study. This difference is presented in Table 10 and Figure 10 below.

Table 10

The Difference between Reported use of Intuition score of US male managers with between 6 and 10 years management experience and US male managers with 5 years or less management experience.

Variable	N	Minimum	Maximum	Mean	Std. Deviation
SCUS5	9	1	10	7	2.692582404
SCUS4	2	8	11	9.5	2.121320344

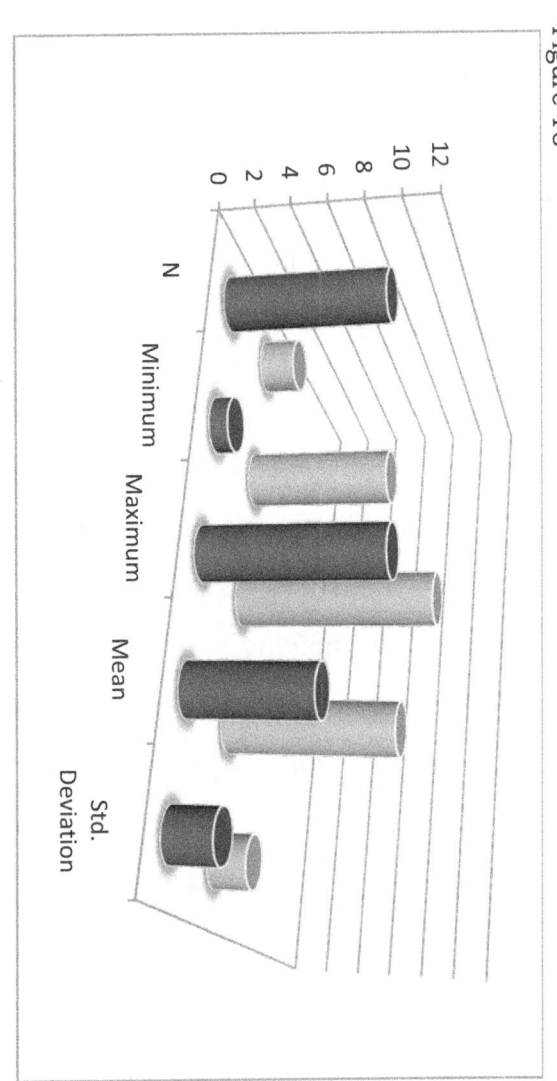

Figure 10

Finding 2.4: US male managers with between 11 and 20 years use of intuition in decision making is lower than US male managers with 5 years or less . Mean scores of US male managers with between 11 and 20 years is 7.2857; US male managers with 5 years or less is 9.5. Significance is at the .010 level.

This finding show that fairly experienced United States male managers who participated in the study used less intuitive right brain decision making skills than barely experienced United States male managers who participated in the study. This difference is presented in Table 11 and Figure 11 below.

Table 11

The Difference between Reported use of Intuition score of US male managers with between 11 and 20 years management experience and US male managers with 5 years or less management experience.

Variable	N	Minimum	Maximum	Mean	Std. Deviation
SCUS6	14	4	11	7.285714286	2.49394872
SCUS4	2	8	11	9.5	2.121320344

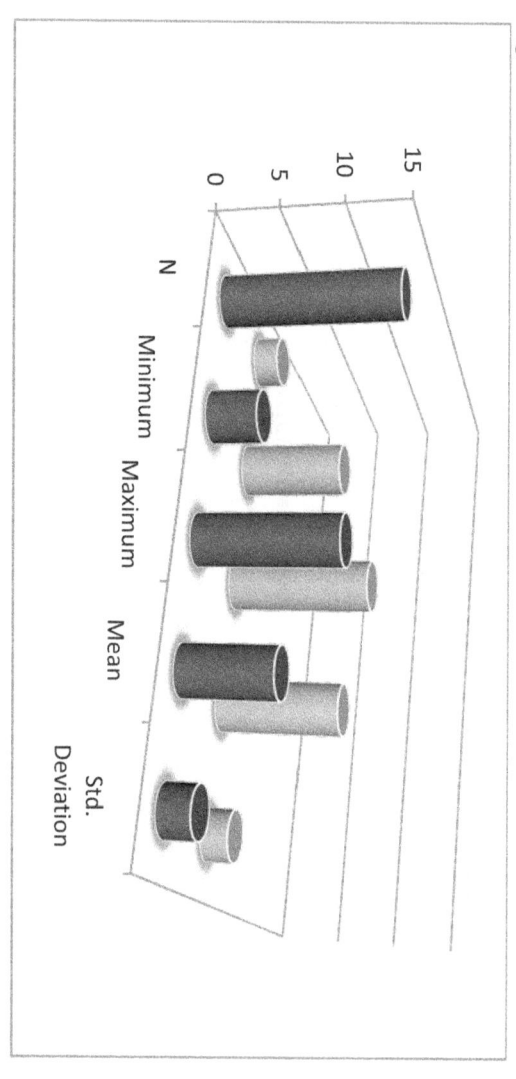

Figure 11

Finding 2.5: US male managers with over 20 years' use of intuition in decision making is lower than US male managers with 5 years or less. Mean scores of US male managers with over 20 years is 7.187; US male managers with 5 years or less is 9.5. Significance is at the .010 level.

This finding show that well experienced US male managers who participated in the study used less intuitive right brain decision making skills than barely experienced US male managers who participated in the study. This difference is presented in Table 12 below.

Table 12

The Difference between Reported use of Intuition score of US male managers with over 20 years management experience and US male managers with 5 years or less management experience.

Variable	N	Minimum	Maximum	Mean	Std. Deviation
SCUS7	16	4	10	7.1875	1.939716474
SCUS4	2	8	11	9.5	2.121320344

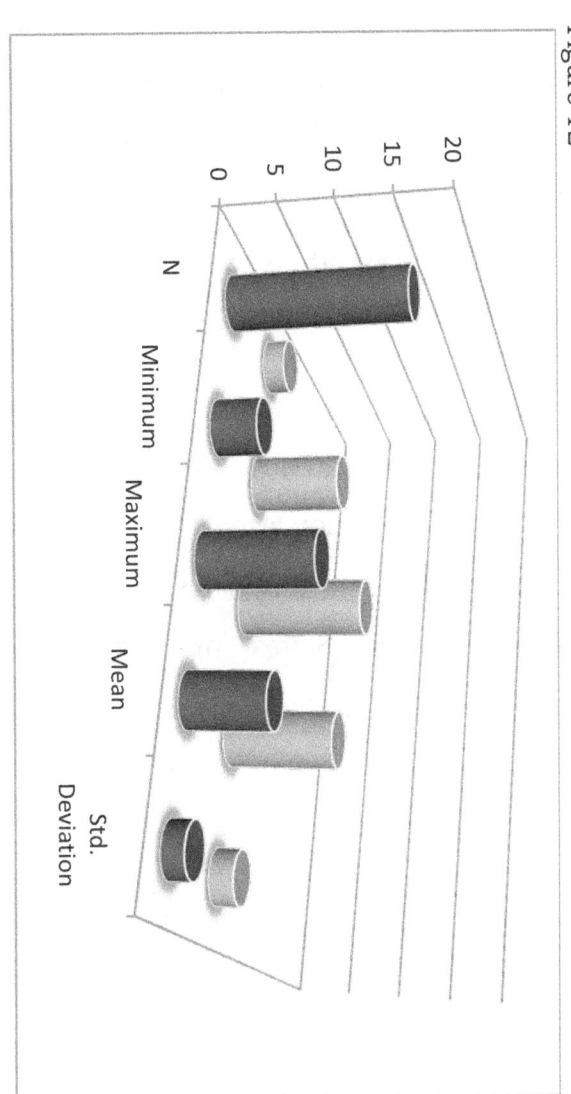

Figure 12

Finding 2.6: US managers with between 11 and 20 years use of intuition in decision making is higher than US managers with 5 years or less . Mean scores of US managers with between 11 and 20 years is 7.4; US managers with 5 years or less is 6.93478. Significance is at the .009 level.

This finding show that fairly experienced United States managers who participated in the study used more intuitive right brain decision making skills than barely experienced United States managers who participated in the study. This difference is presented in Table 13 and Figure 13 below.

Table 13

The Difference between Reported use of Intuition score of US managers with between 11 and 20 years management experience and US managers with 5 years or less management experience.

Variable	N	Minimum	Maximum	Mean	Std. Deviation
USSC3	20	3	11	7.4	2.43656
USSC	46	2	12	6.93478	2.18481

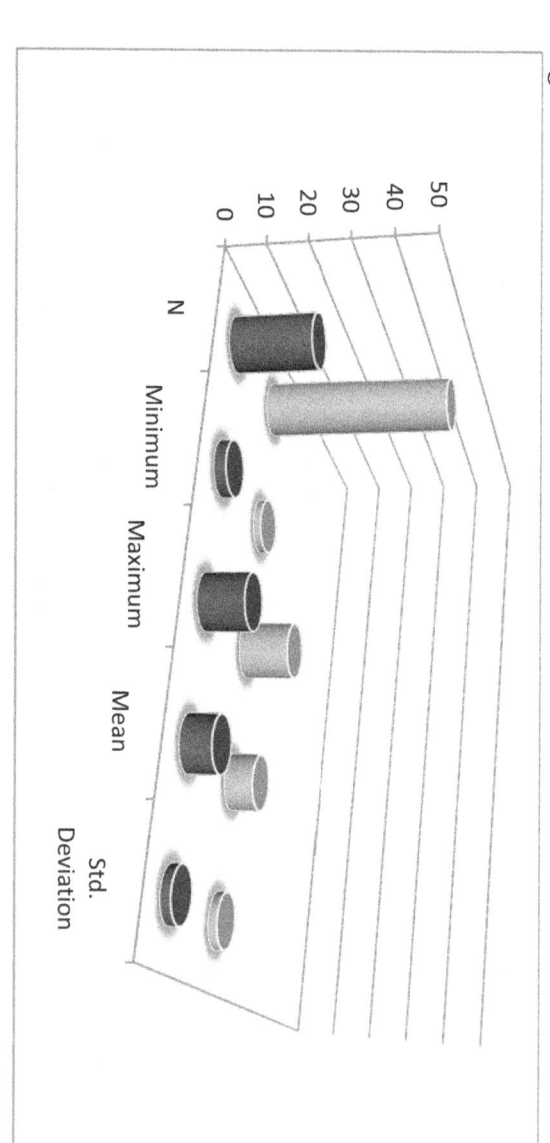

Figure 13

Finding 2.7: US managers with more than 20 years' use of intuition in decision making is higher than US managers with between 6 and 10 years. Mean scores of US managers with more than 20 years is 7.44; US managers with between 6 and 10 years is 7.0. Significance is at the .046 level.

This finding show that well experienced US managers who participated in the study used more intuitive right brain decision making skills than moderately experienced US managers who participated in the study. This difference is presented in Table 14 below.

Table 14

The Difference between Reported use of Intuition score of US managers with more than 20 years management experience and US managers with between 6 and 10 years management experience.

Variable	N	Minimum	Maximum	Mean	Std. Deviation
USSC4	18	4	11	7.4444	2.03563
USSC2	16	1	10	7	2.3944

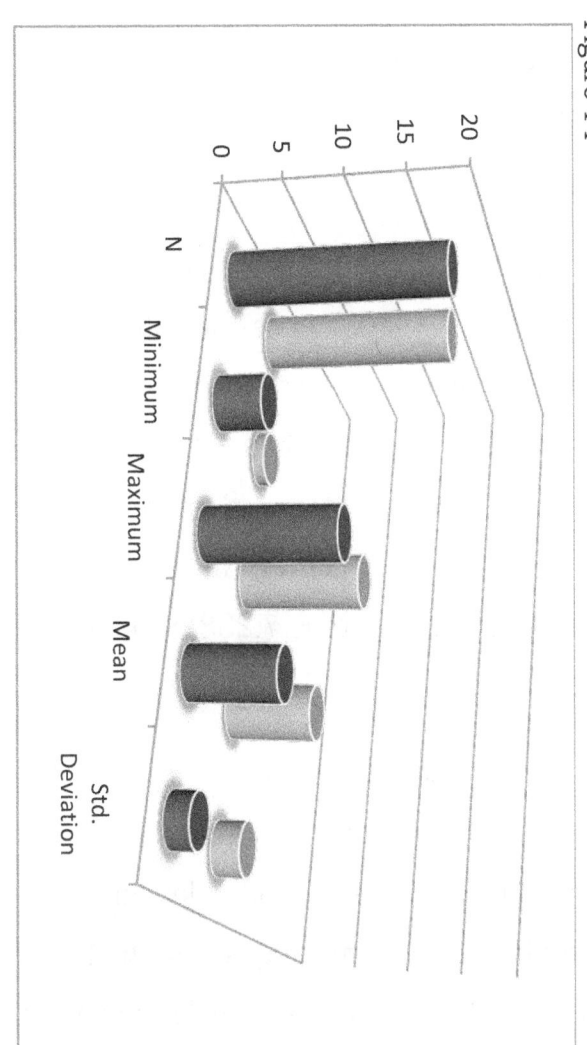

Figure 14

SEX AND BRAIN USAGE

Research Question 3: What is the relationship between sex and reported use of intuition in decision making?

Finding 3.1: US male managers with more than 20 years' use of intuition in decision making is lower than US female managers with between 6 and 10 years. Mean scores of US male managers with more than 20 years is 7.1875; US female managers with between 6 and 10 years is 7.238. Significance is at.013 level.

This finding show that highly experienced United States male managers who participated in the study utilize less intuitive right brain decision making skills than less experienced United States female managers who participated in the study. This difference is presented in Table 15 below.

Table 15

The Difference between Reported use of Intuition score of US male managers with more than 20 years management experience and US female managers with between 6 and 10 years management experience.

Variable	N	Minimum	Maximum	Mean	Std. Deviation
SCUS7	16	4	10	7.1875	1.939716474
SCUS1	21	3	11	7.23809523	2.071346468

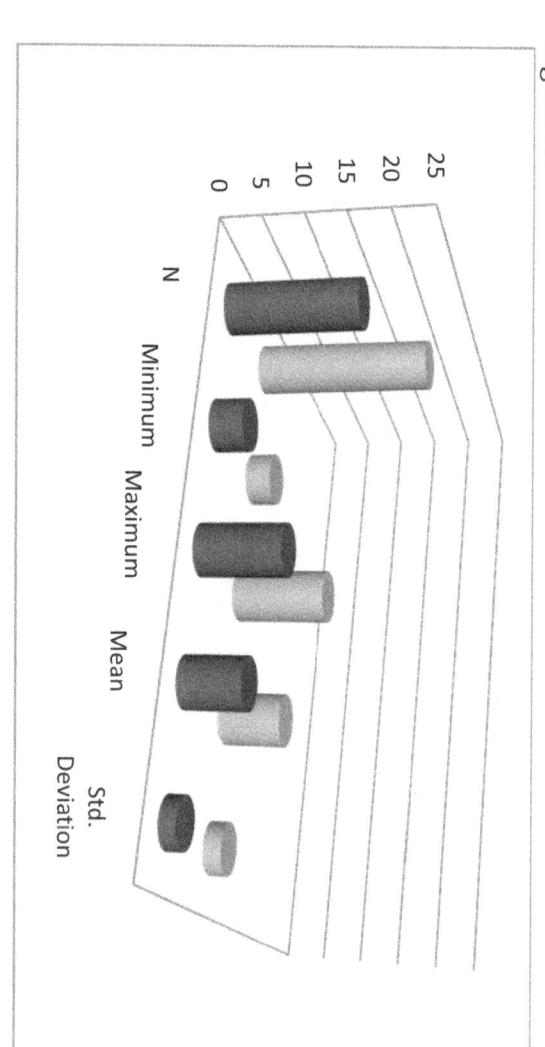

Figure 15

Finding 3.2: Hong Kong female managers with between 6 and 10 years' use of intuition in decision making is higher than Hong Kong female managers with between 11 and 20 years. Mean scores of female managers with between 6 and 10 years in Hong Kong is 6.3809; Hong Kong female managers with between 11 and 20 years is 6.333. Significance is at the .032 level.

This finding show that moderately experienced Hong Kong female managers who participated in the study used more intuitive right brain decision making skills than more experienced Hong Kong female managers who participated in the study. This difference is presented in Table 16 and Figure 16 below.

Table 16

The Difference between Reported use of Intuition score of Hong Kong Female managers with between 6 and 10 years management experience and Hong Kong female managers with between 11 and 20 years management experience.

Variable	N	Minimum	Maximum	Mean	Std. Deviation
SCHK1	21	3	10	6.380952381	2.01186954
SCHK2	12	2	10	6.333333333	2.605355789

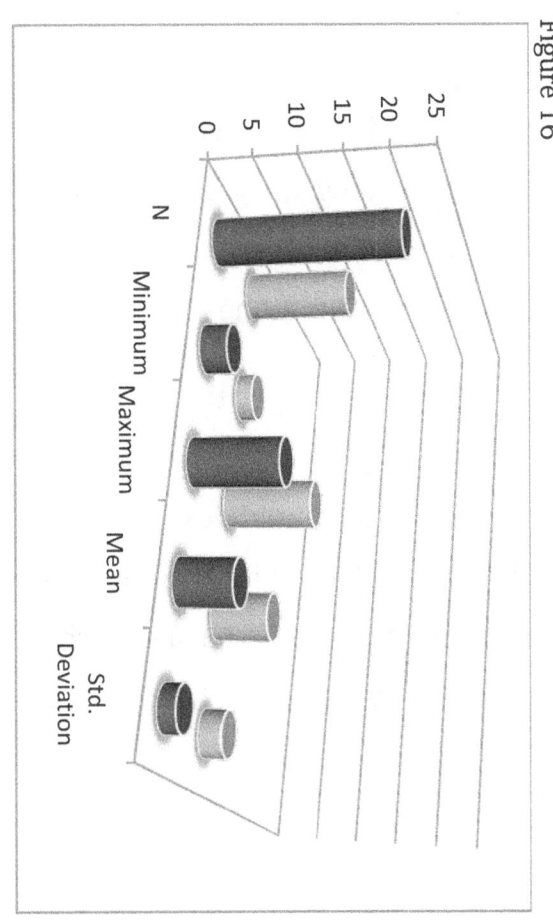

Figure 16

Finding3.3: Female managers in Hong Kong with 5 years or less use of intuition in decision making is lower than US male managers with 5 years or less. Mean scores of Female managers in Hong Kong with 5 years or less is 7.1; US male managers with 5 years or less is 9.5. Significance is at the .010 level.

This finding show that barely experienced Hong Kong female managers who participated in the study used less intuitive right brain decision making skills than equally experienced United States male managers who participated in the study. This difference is presented in Table 17 and Figure 17 below.

Table 17

The Difference between Reported use of Intuition score of Female managers in Hong Kong with 5 years or less management experience and US male managers with 5 years or less management experience.

Variable	N	Minimum	Maximum	Mean	Std. Deviation
SCHK	20	3	11	7.1	2.468752082
SCUS4	2	8	11	9.5	2.121320344

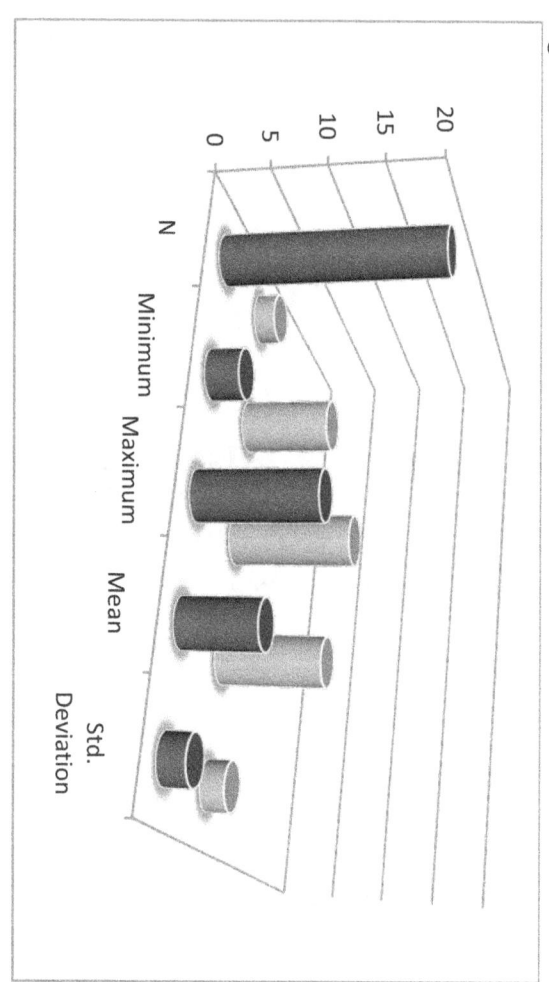

Figure 17

Finding 3.4: US female managers with 5 years or less' use of intuition in decision making is lower than US male managers with 5 years or less. Mean scores of US female managers with 5 years or less is 6.35; US male managers with 5 years or less is 9.5. Significance is at the .010 level.

This finding show that barely experienced United States female managers who participated in the study used less intuitive right brain decision making skills than equally experienced US male managers who participated in the study. This difference is presented in Table 18 and Figure 18 below.

Table 18

The Difference between Reported use of Intuition score of US female managers with 5 years or less management experience and US male managers with 5 years or less management experience.

Variable	N	Minimum	Maximum	Mean	Std. Deviation
SCUS	20	2	10	6.35	2.1830
SCUS4	2	8	11	9.5	2.121320344

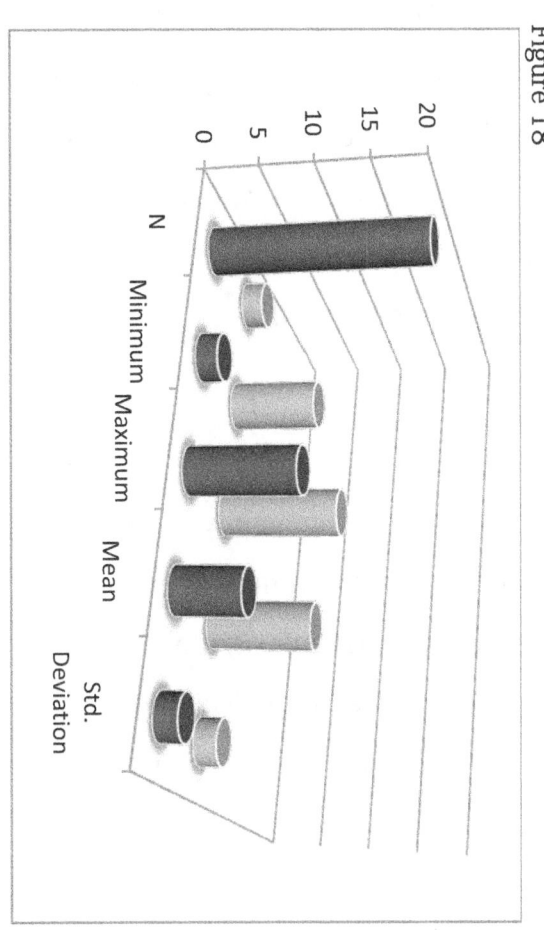

Figure 18

Finding 3.5: US female managers with between 6 and 10 years use of intuition in decision making is lower than US male managers with 5 years or less . Mean scores of US female managers with between 6 and 10 years is 7.238; US male managers with 5 years or less is 9.5. Significance is at the .010 level.

This finding show that moderately experienced United States female managers who participated in the study used less intuitive right brain decision making skills than less experienced United States male managers who participated in the study. This difference is presented in Table 19 and Figure 19 below.

Table 19

The Difference between Reported use of Intuition score of US female managers with between 6 and 10 years management experience and US male managers with 5 years or less management experience.

Variable	N	Minimum	Maximum	Mean	Std. Deviation
SCUS1	21	3	11	7.238095238	2.071346468
SCUS4	2	8	11	9.5	2.121320344

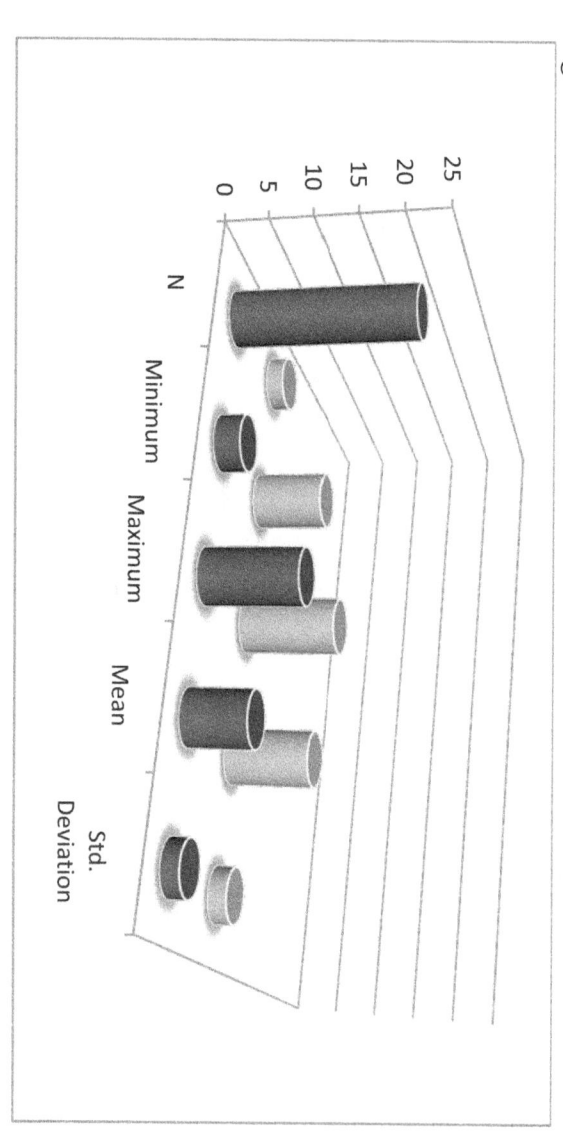

Figure 19

Finding 3.6: US female managers with between 11 and 20 years use of intuition in decision making is lower than US male managers with 5 years or less . Mean scores of US female managers with between 11 and 20 years is 7.0 US male managers with 5 years or less is 9.5. Significance is at the .010 level.

This finding show that fairly experienced US female managers who participated in the study used less intuitive right brain decision making skills than barely experienced United States male managers who participated in the study. This difference is presented in Table 20 and Figure 20 below.

Table 20

The Difference between Reported use of Intuition score of US female managers with between 11 and 20 years management experience and US male managers with 5 years or less management experience.

Variable	N	Minimum	Maximum	Mean	Std. Deviation
SCUS2	7	3	9	7	2.16024689
SCUS4	2	8	11	9.5	2.121320344

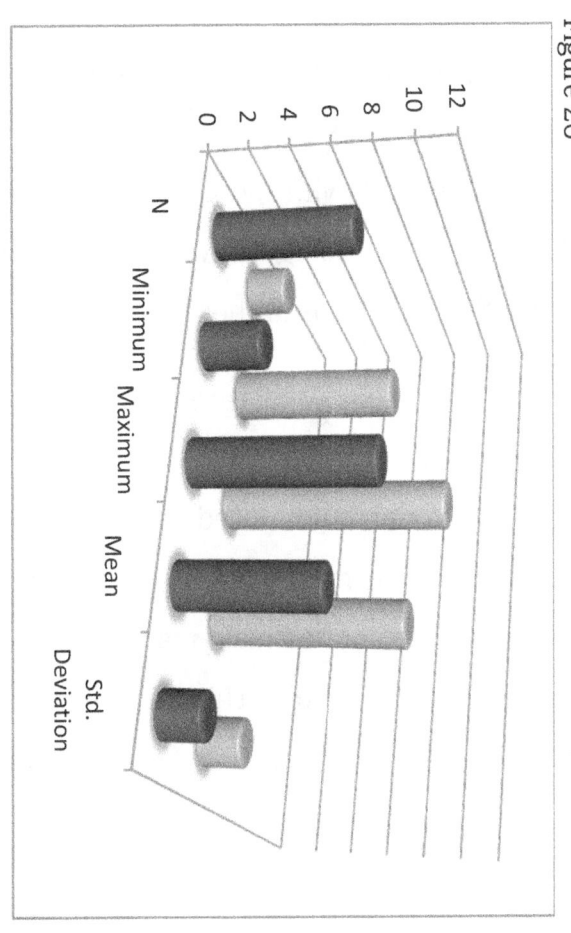

Figure 20

Finding 3.7: US female managers with more than 20 years' use of intuition in decision making is lower than US male managers with 5 years or less. Mean scores of US female managers with more than 20 years is 7.666; US male managers with 5 years or less is 9.5. Significance is at the .010 level.

This finding show that well experienced United States female managers who participated in the study used less intuitive right brain decision making skills than barely experienced United States male managers who participated in the study. This difference is presented in Table 21 and Figure 21 below.

Table 21

The Difference between Reported use of Intuition score of US female managers with more than 20 years management experience and US male managers with 5 years or less management experience.

Variable	N	Minimum	Maximum	Mean	Std. Deviation
SCUS3	6	3	10	7.666666667	2.503331114
SCUS4	2	8	11	9.5	2.121320344

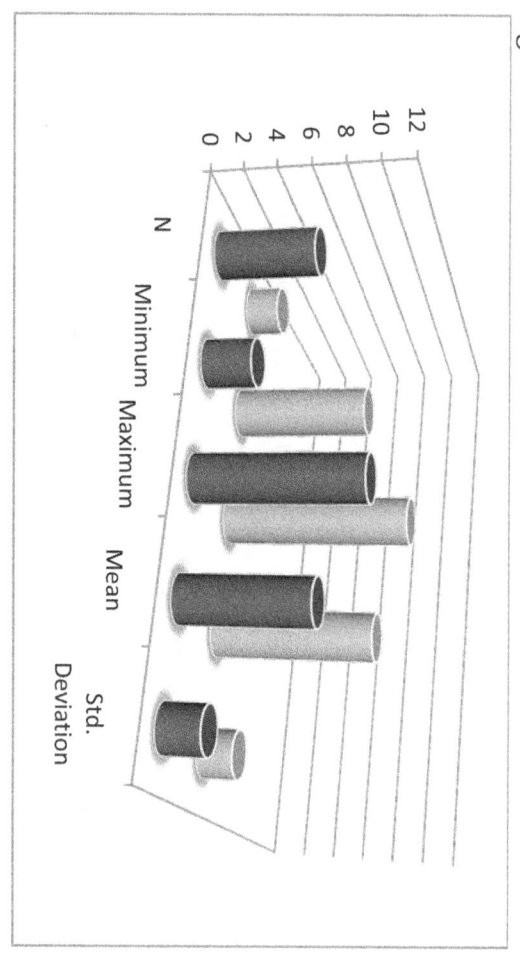

Figure 21

Finding 3.8: US male executives' use of intuition in decision making is lower than US female managers' use. Mean scores of US male executives is 7.388; US female managers' is 7.461. Significance is at the .005 level.

This finding show that United States male executives who participated in the study used less intuitive right brain decision making skills than United States female managers who participated in the study. This difference is presented in Table 22 and Figure 22 below.

Table 22

The Difference between Reported use of Intuition score of US male executives and US female managers.

Variable	N	Minimum	Maximum	Mean	Std. Deviation
SCUS6	8	4	11	7.3888	1.9444
SCUS1	13	4	12	7.4615	2.33150

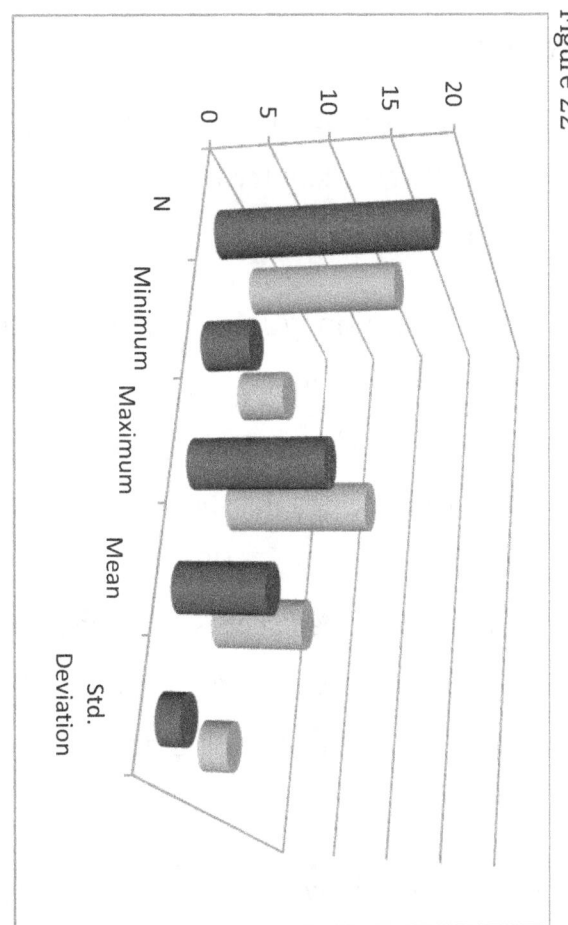

Figure 22

BRAIN USAGE AND COUNTRY OF OPERATION

Research Question 4: What is the relationship between country of operation and use of intuition in decision making?

Finding 4.1: Hong Kong administrative managers' use of intuition in decision making is lower than US administrative managers' use. Mann-Whitney U results showed the mean rank of Hong Kong is 13.17; US administrative managers is 20.94. Mean scores of Hong Kong administrative managers is 6.333; US administrative managers is 8.11. Significance is at the .023 level.

This finding show that US administrative managers who participated in the study used more intuitive right brain decision making skills than Hong Kong administrative managers who participated in the study. This difference is presented in Table 23 and Figure 23 below.

Table 23

The Difference between Reported use of Intuition score of Hong Kong Administrative Managers and US Administrative Managers.

Variable 1	N	MS	SD	Minimum	Maximum
US Managers	9	8.1111	1.36423	7.00	11.00
HK Managers	21	6.3333	2.28765	2.00	11.00

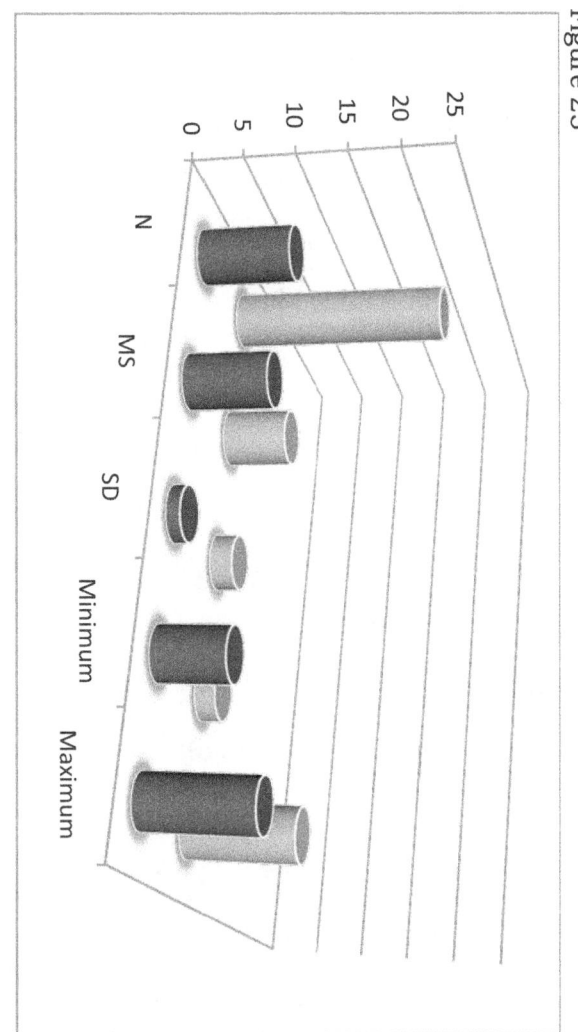

Figure 23

Finding 4.2: Hong Kong Supervisors with 10 years or less' use of intuition in decision making is lower than US supervisors with more than 10 years. Mean scores of Supervisors with 10 years or less in Hong Kong is 6.6363; US supervisors with over 10 years is 8.00. Significance is at the 0.01 level.

This finding show that moderately experienced Hong Kong supervisors who participated in the study used less intuitive right brain decision making skills than more experienced United States supervisors who participated in the study. This difference is presented in Table 24 and Figure 24 below.

Table 24

The Difference between Reported use of Intuition score of Hong Kong Supervisors with 10 years or less management experience and US supervisors with over 10 years management experience.

Variable	N	Minimum	Maximum	Mean	Std. Deviation
SCHK	22	3	11	6.6363	2.32062
SCUS1	2	7	9	8	1.4142

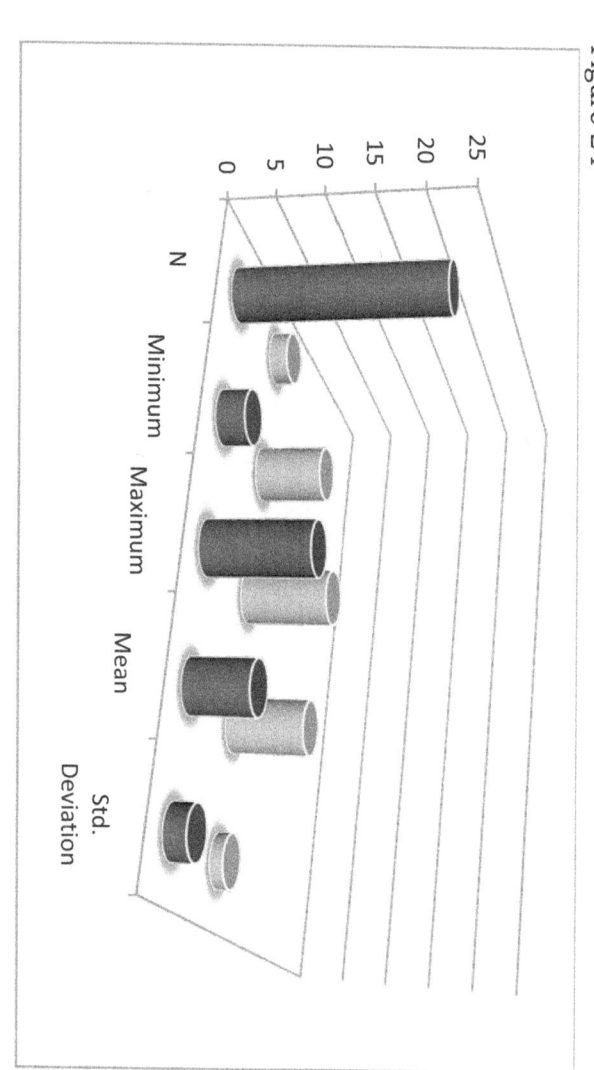

Figure 24

Finding 4.3: Hong Kong managers with 10 years or less' use of intuition in decision making is lower than US supervisors with over 10 years. Mean scores of Managers with 10 years or less in Hong Kong is 6.8636; US supervisors with over 10 years is 8.00. Significance is at the 0.01 level.

This finding show that moderately experienced Hong Kong managers who participated in the study used less intuitive right brain decision making skills than more experienced United States supervisors who participated in the study. This difference is presented in Table 25 and Figure 25 below.

Table 25

The Difference between Reported use of Intuition score of Hong Kong Managers with 10 years or less management experience and US supervisors with over 10 years management experience.

Variable	N	Minimum	Maximum	Mean	Std. Deviation
SCHK2	22	4	11	6.8636	2.2739
SCUS1	2	7	9	8	1.4142

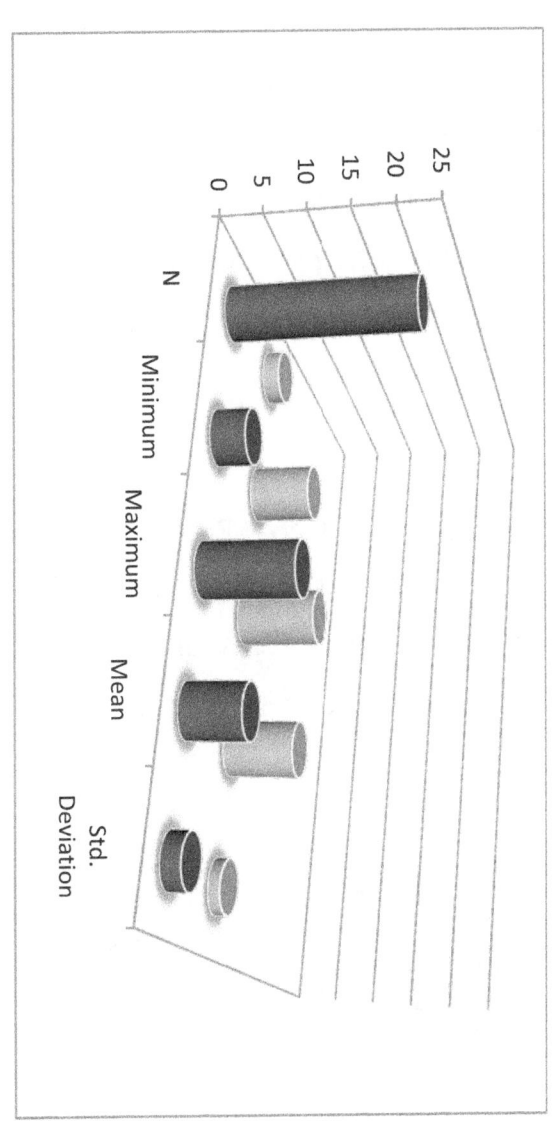

Figure 25

Finding 4.4: Hong Kong managers with more than 10 years' use of intuition in decision making is lower than US supervisors with over 10 years. Mean scores of managers with more than 10 years in Hong Kong is 7.6666; US supervisors with over 10 years is 8.00. Significance is at the 0.01 level.

This finding show that experienced HK managers who participated in the study used less intuitive right brain decision making skills than equally experienced US supervisors who participated in the study. This difference is presented in Table 26 and Figure 26 below.

Table 26

The Difference between Reported use of Intuition score of Hong Kong Managers with more than 10 years management experience and US supervisors with over 10 years management experience.

Variable	N	Minimum	Maximum	Mean	Std. Deviation
SCHK3	9	5	11	7.6666	1.93649
SCUS1	2	7	9	8	1.4142

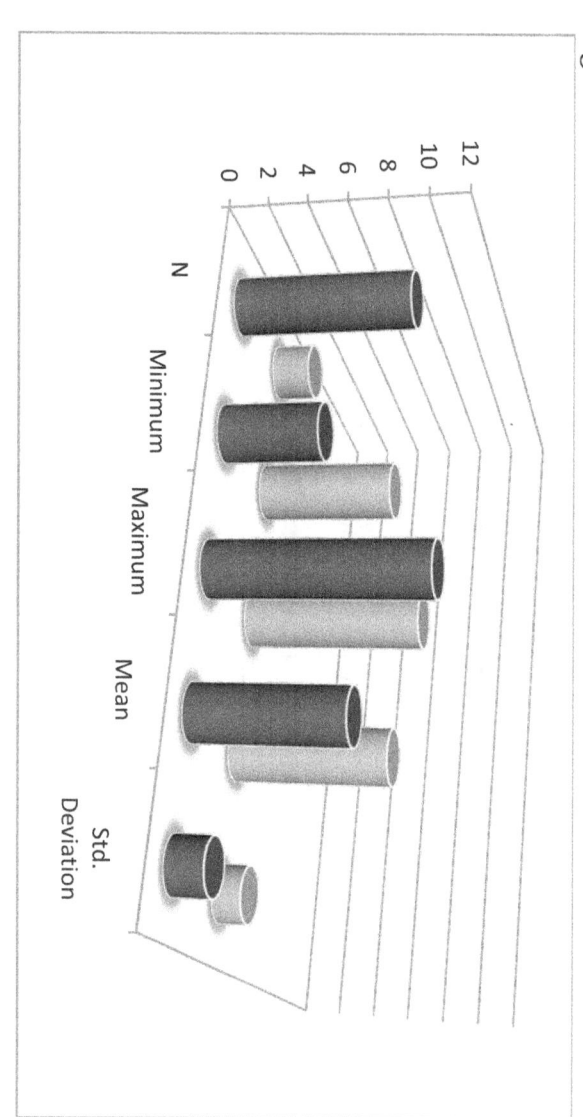

Figure 26

Finding 4.5: Hong Kong Executives with 10 years or less' use of intuition in decision making is lower than US supervisors with over 10 years. Mean scores of Executives with 10 years or less in Hong Kong is 7.125; US supervisors with over 10 years is 8.00. Significance is at the 0.01 level.

This finding show that moderately experienced Hong Kong executives who participated in the study used less intuitive right brain decision making skills than more experienced United States supervisors who participated in the study. This difference is presented in Table 27 and Figure 27 below.

Table 27

The Difference between Reported use of Intuition score of Hong Kong Executives with 10 years or less management experience and US supervisors with over 10 years management experience.

Variable	N	Minimum	Maximum	Mean	Std. Deviation
SCHK4	16	2	11	7.125	2.6044
SCUS1	2	7	9	8	1.4142

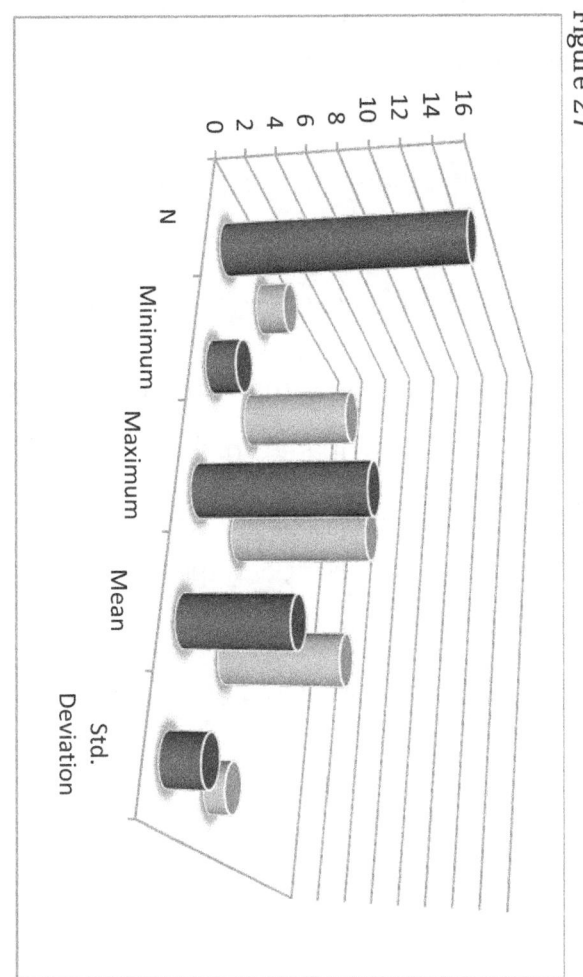

Figure 27

Finding 4.6: Hong Kong executives with more than 10 years' use of intuition in decision making is lower than United States supervisors with over 10 years. Mean scores of Executives with more than 10 years in Hong Kong is 7.25; US supervisors with over 10 years is 8.00. Significance is at the 0.01 level.

This finding show that experienced HK executives who participated in the study used less intuitive right brain decision making skills than more experienced US supervisors who participated in the study. This difference is presented in Table 28 and Figure 28 below.

Table 28

The Difference between Reported use of Intuition score of Hong Kong Executives with more than 10 years management experience and US supervisors with over 10 years management experience.

Variable	N	Minimum	Maximum	Mean	Std. Deviation
SCHK5	12	3	11	7.25	2.5980
SCUS1	2	7	9	8	1.4142

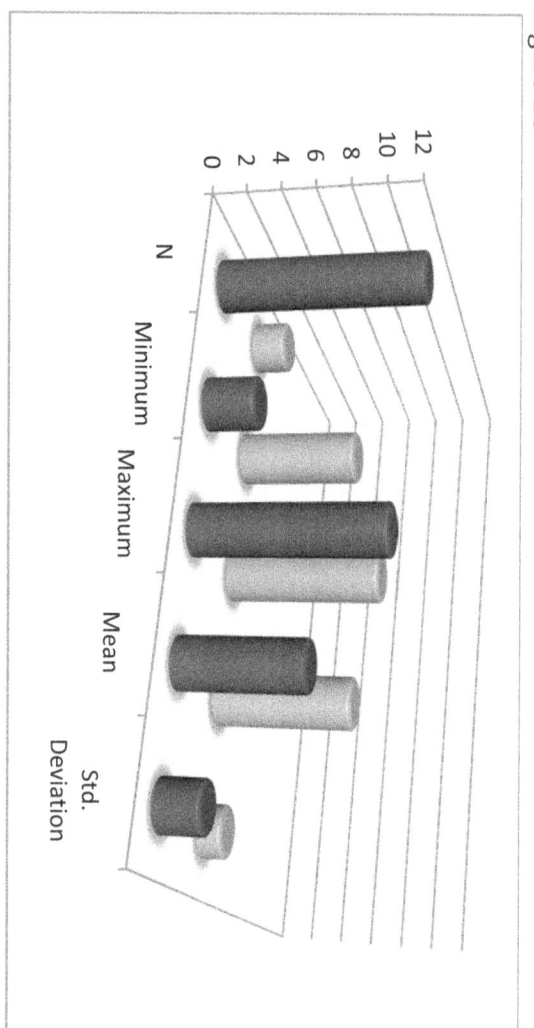

Figure 28

Finding 4.7: Hong Kong business owners with 10 years or less' use of intuition in decision making is lower than US supervisors with over 10 years. Mean scores of Business owners with 10 years or less in Hong Kong is 6.00; US supervisors with over 10 years is 8.00. Significance is at the 0.01 level.

This finding show that moderately experienced Hong Kong business owners who participated in the study used less intuitive right brain decision making skills than more experienced United States supervisors who participated in the study. This difference is presented in Table 29 and Figure 29 below.

Table 29

The Difference between Reported use of Intuition score of Hong Kong Business owners with 10 years or less management experience and US supervisors with over 10 years management experience.

Variable	N	Minimum	Maximum	Mean	Std. Deviation
SCHK6	9	3	11	6	2.5
SCUS1	2	7	9	8	1.4142

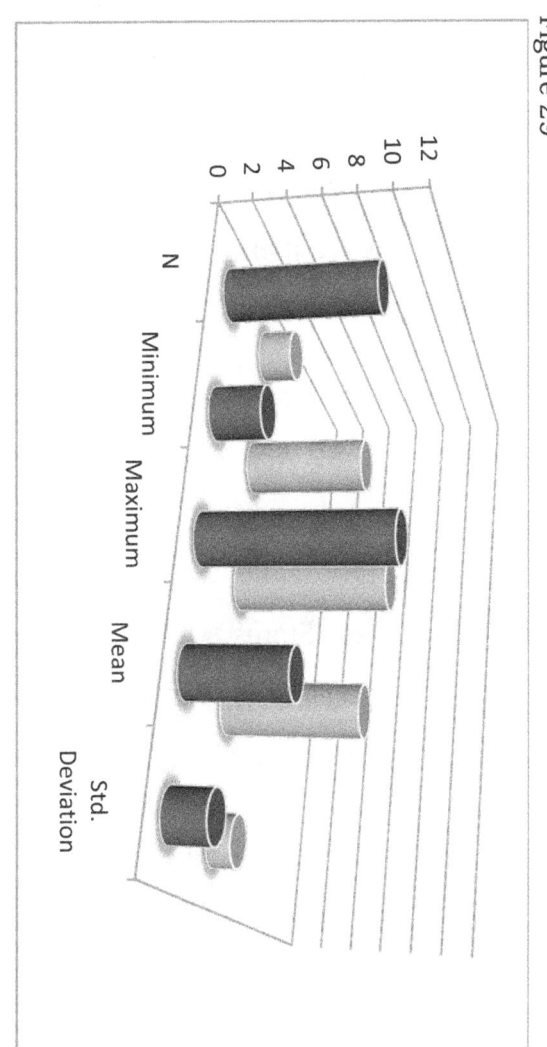

Figure 29

Finding 4.8: Hong Kong business owners with over 10 years' use of intuition in decision making is lower than United States supervisors with over 10 years. Mean scores of Business owners with over 10 years in Hong Kong is 7.7142; US supervisors with over 10 years is 8.00. Significance is at the 0.01 level.

This finding show that experienced Hong Kong business owners who participated in the study used less intuitive right brain decision making skills than equally experienced United States supervisors who participated in the study. This difference is presented in Table 30 and Figure 30 below.

Table 30

The Difference between Reported use of Intuition score of Hong Kong Business owners with over 10 years management experience and US supervisors with over 10 years management experience.

Variable	N	Minimum	Maximum	Mean	Std. Deviation
SCHK7	7	5	12	7.7142	2.69037
SCUS1	2	7	9	8	1.4142

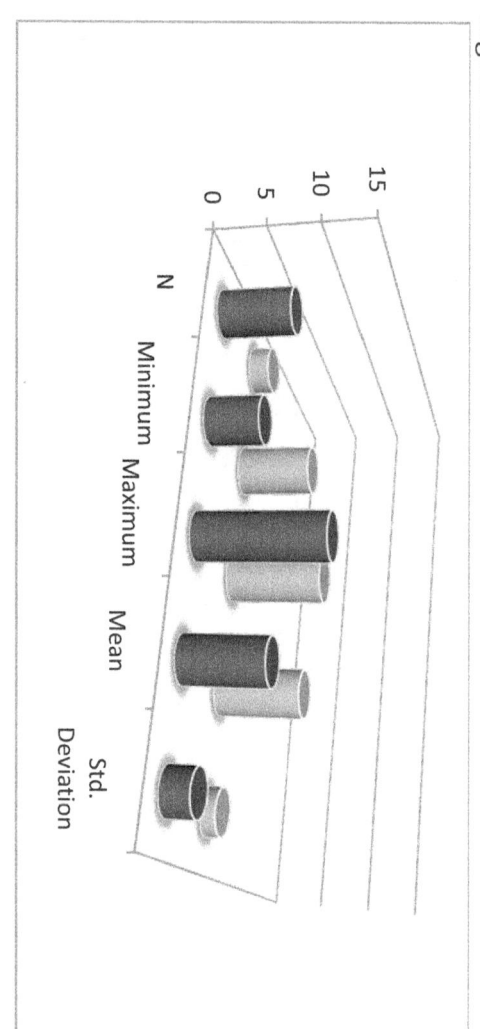

Figure 30

Finding 4.9: Hong Kong Business owners with over 10 years' use of intuition in decision making is higher than US managers with 10 years or less. Mean scores of Business owners with over 10 years in Hong Kong is 7.7142; US managers with 10 years or less is 7.1304. Significance is at the 0.01 level.

This finding show that experienced HK business owners who participated in the study used more intuitive right brain decision making skills than less experienced US managers who participated in the study. This difference is presented in Table 31 and Figure 31 below.

Table 31

The Difference between Reported use of Intuition score of Hong Kong Business owners with over 10 years management experience and US managers with 10 years or less management experience.

Variable	N	Minimum	Maximum	Mean	Std. Deviation
SCHK7	7	5	12	7.7142	2.69037
SCUS2	23	1	12	7.1304	2.5281

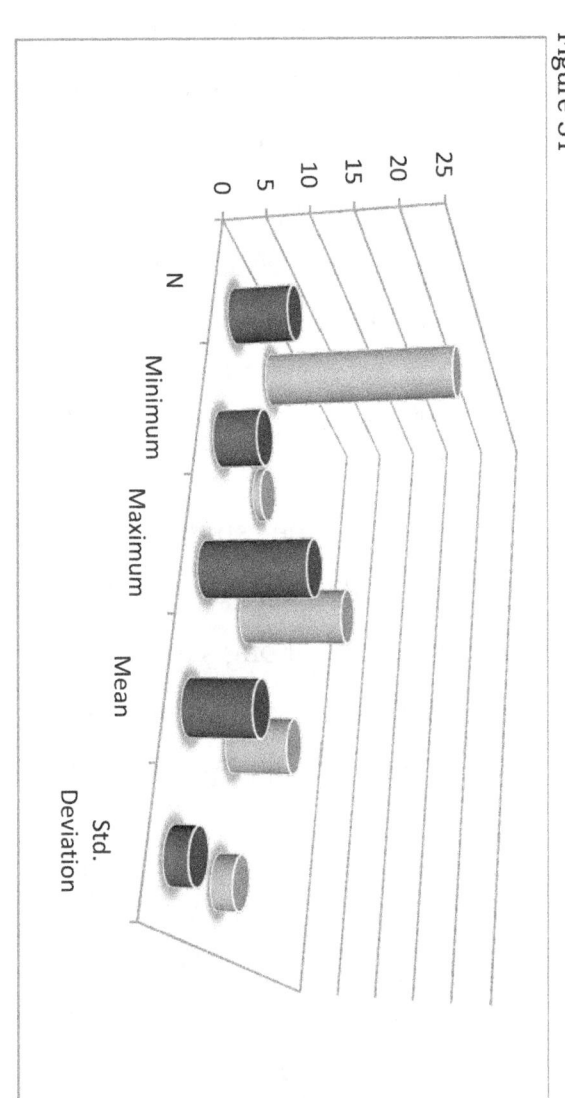

Figure 31

Finding 4.10: US business owners with 10 years or less' use of intuition in decision making is higher than Hong Kong supervisors with over 10 years. Mean scores of United States business owners with 10 years or less is 8.00; Hong Kong Supervisors with over 10 years is 6.00. Significance is at the 0.01 level.

This finding show that moderately experienced United States business owners who participated in the study used more intuitive right brain decision making skills than more experienced Hong Kong supervisors who participated in the study. This difference is presented in Table 32 and Figure 32 below.

Table 32

The Difference between Reported use of Intuition score of US business owners with 10 years or less management experience and Hong Kong supervisors with over 10 years management experience.

Variable	N	Minimum	Maximum	Mean	Std. Deviation
SCUS6	10	6	10	8	1.49071
SCHK1	3	5	8	6	1.7320

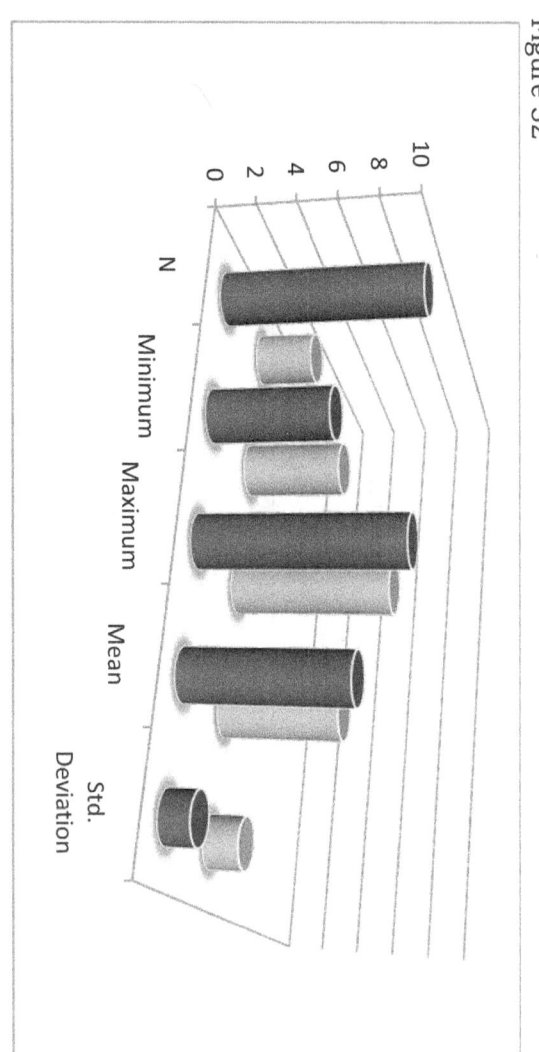

Figure 32

Finding 4.11: Female managers in Hong Kong with between 6 and 10 years use of intuition in decision making is lower than US male managers with 5 years or less . Mean scores of Female managers in Hong Kong with between 6 and 10 years is 6.380; United States male managers with 5 years or less is 9.5. Significance is at the .010 level.

This finding show that moderately experienced Hong Kong female managers who participated in the study used less intuitive right brain decision making skills than less experienced United States male managers who participated in the study. This difference is presented in Table 33 and Figure 33 below.

Table 33

The Difference between Reported use of Intuition score of Female managers in Hong Kong with between 6 and 10 years management experience and US male managers with 5 years or less management experience.

Variable	N	Minimum	Maximum	Mean	Std. Deviation
SCHK1	21	3	10	6.380952381	2.01186954
SCUS4	2	8	11	9.5	2.12132034

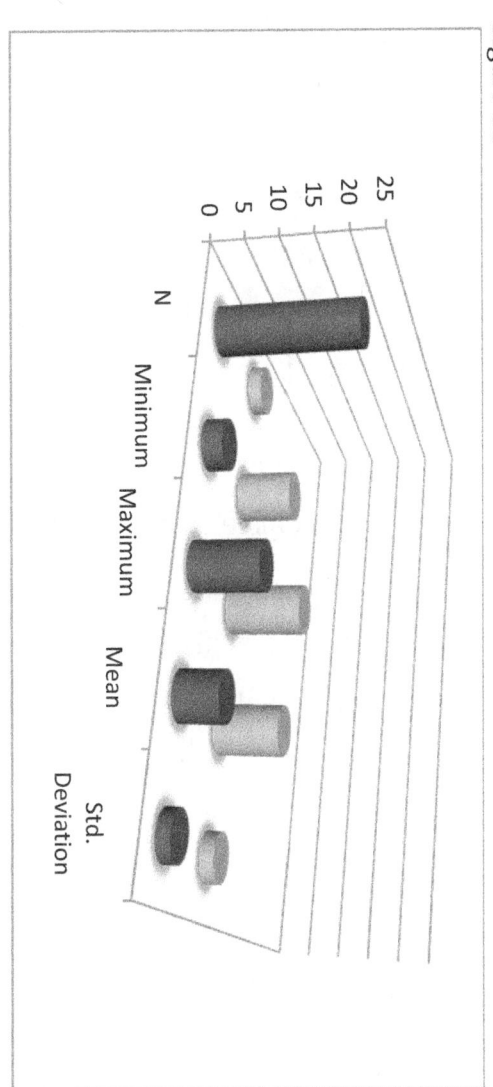

Figure 33

Finding 4.12: Female managers in Hong Kong with between 11 and 20 years use of intuition in decision making is lower than US male managers with 5 years or less . Mean scores of Female managers in Hong Kong with between 11 and 20 years is 6.333; US male managers with 5 years or less is 9.5. Significance is at the .010 level.

This finding show that fairly experienced Hong Kong female managers who participated in the study used less intuitive right brain decision making skills than barely experienced United States male managers who participated in the study. This difference is presented in Table 34 and Figure 34 below.

Table 34

The Difference between Reported use of Intuition score of Female managers in Hong Kong with between 11 and 20 years management experience and US male managers with 5 years or less management experience.

Variable	N	Minimum	Maximum	Mean	Std. Deviation
SCHK2	12	2	10	6.333333333	2.60535789
SCUS4	2	8	11	9.5	2.121320344

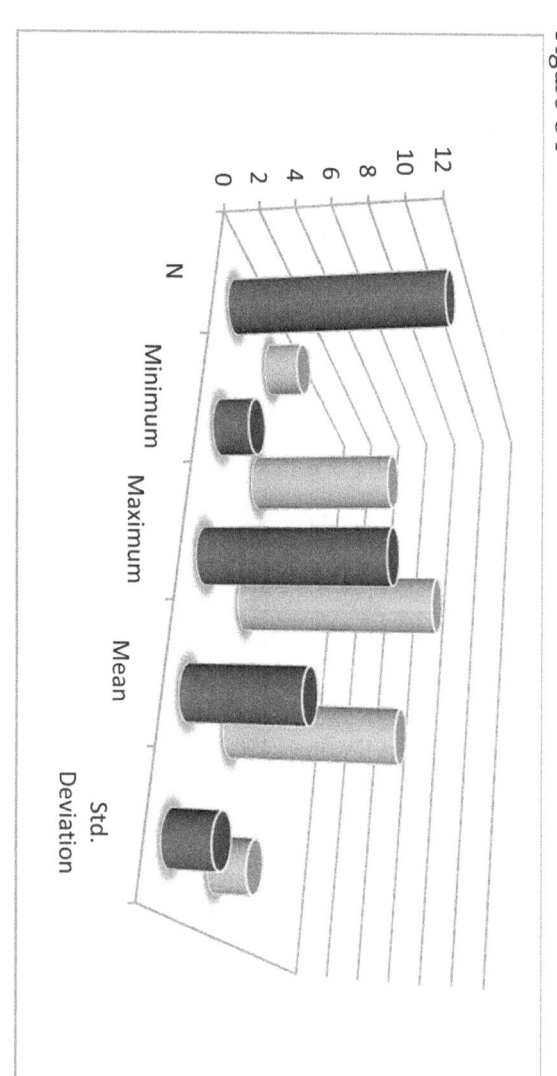

Figure 34

Finding 4.13: Female managers in Hong Kong with more than 20 years' use of intuition in decision making is lower than US male managers with 5 years or less. Mean scores of Female managers in Hong Kong with more than 20 years is 6.875; US male managers with 5 years or less is 9.5. Significance is at the .010 level.

This finding show that well experienced Hong Kong female managers who participated in the study used less intuitive right brain decision making skills than barely experienced United States male managers who participated in the study. This difference is presented in Table 35 and Figure 35 below.

Table 35

The Difference between Reported use of Intuition score of Female managers in Hong Kong with more than 20 years management experience and US male managers with 5 years or less management experience.

Variable	N	Minimum	Maximum	Mean	Std. Deviation
SCHK3	8	3	11	6.875	2.6958963352
SCUS4	2	8	11	9.5	2.12132034.4

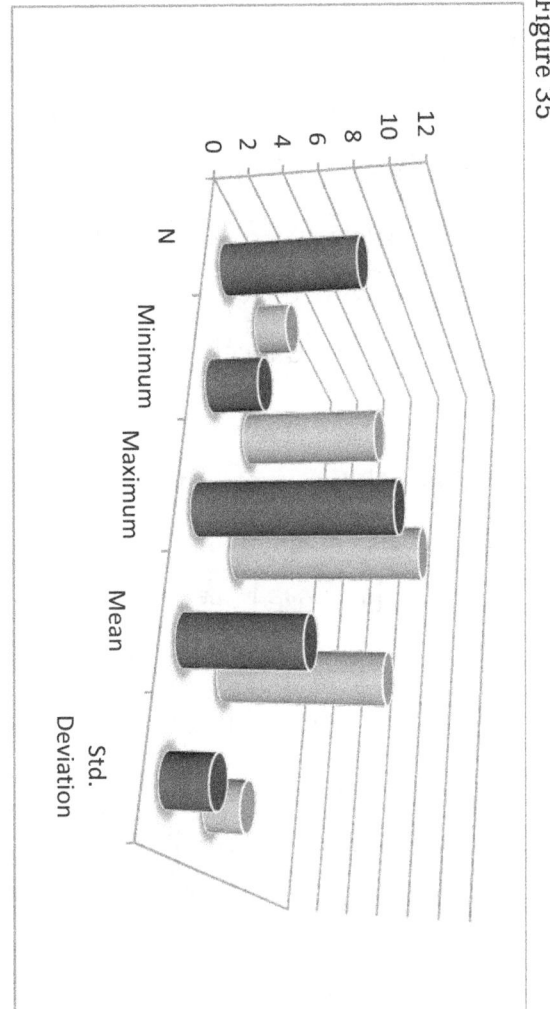

Figure 35

Finding 4.14: Male managers in Hong Kong with between 6 and 10 years use of intuition in decision making is lower than US male managers with 5 years or less . Mean scores of Male managers in Hong Kong with between 6 and 10 years is 7.0625; United States male managers with 5 years or less is 9.5. Significance is at the .010 level.

This finding show that moderately experienced Hong Kong male managers who participated in the study used less intuitive right brain decision making skills than barely experienced United States male managers who participated in the study. This difference is presented in Table 36 and Figure 36 below.

Table 36

The Difference between Reported use of Intuition score of Male managers in Hong Kong with between 6 and 10 years management experience and US male managers with 5 years or less management experience.

Variable	N	Minimum	Maximum	Mean	Std. Deviation
SCHK5	16	3	11	7.0625	2.59406373
SCUS4	2	8	11	9.5	2.121320344

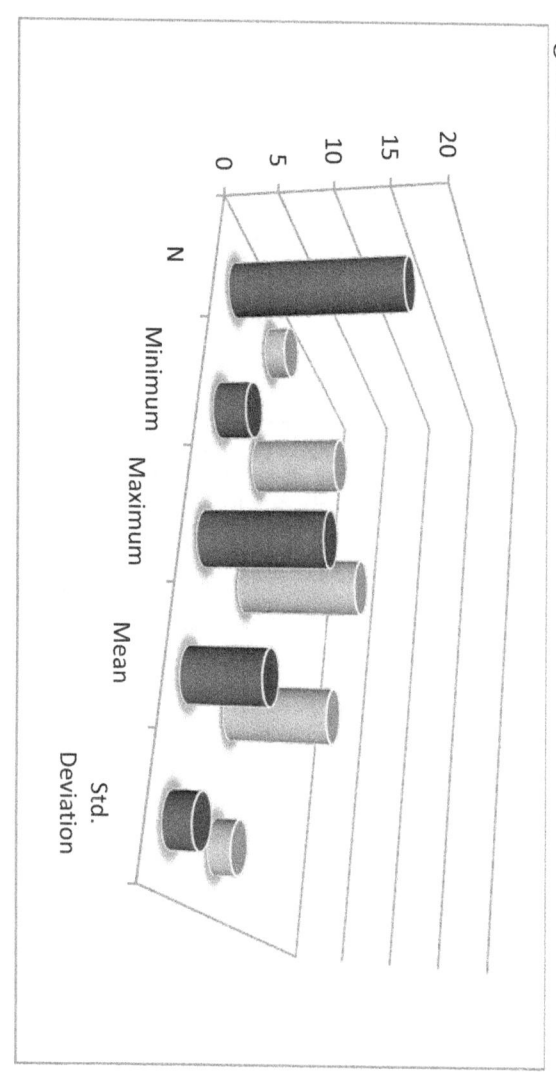

Figure 36

Finding 4.15: Male managers in Hong Kong with between 11 and 20 years use of intuition in decision making is lower than US male managers with 5 years or less . Mean scores of Hong Kong administrative managers is 6.8571; US administrative managers is 9.5. Significance is at the .010 level.

This finding show that fairly experienced Hong Kong male managers who participated in the study used less intuitive right brain decision making skills than barely experienced United States male managers who participated in the study. This difference is presented in Table 37 and Figure 37 below.

Table 37

The Difference between Reported use of Intuition score of Male managers in Hong Kong with between 11 and 20 years management experience and US male managers with 5 years or less management experience.

Variable	N	Minimum	Maximum	Mean	Std. Deviation
SCHK6	14	4	9	6.857142857	1.610405723
SCUS4	2	8	11	9.5	2.121320344

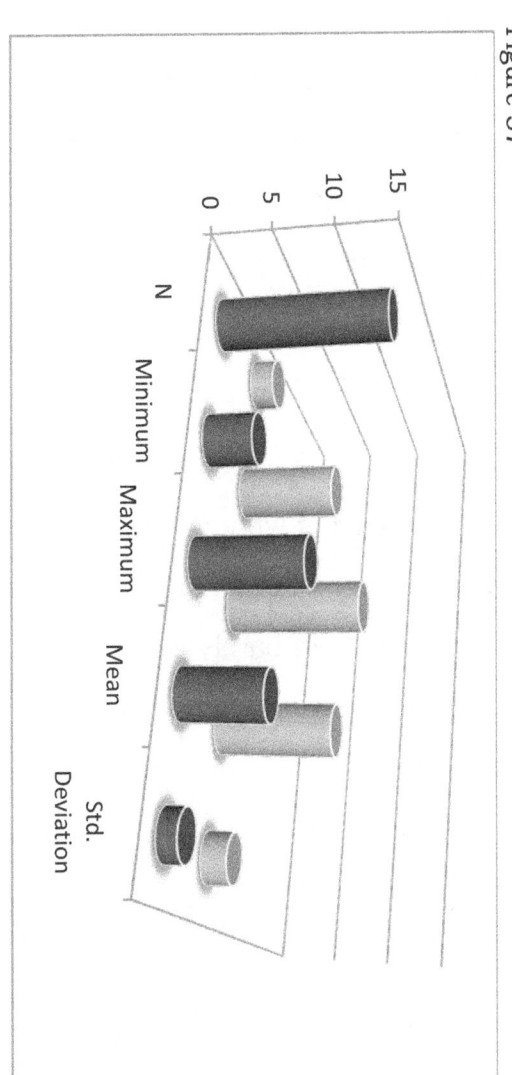

Figure 37

Finding 4.16: Male managers in Hong Kong with more than 20 years' use of intuition in decision making is lower than US male managers with 5 years or less. Mean scores of Male managers in Hong Kong with more than 20 years is 8.125; US male managers with 5 years or less is 9.5. Significance is at the .010 level.

This finding show that well experienced Hong Kong male managers who participated in the study used less intuitive right brain decision making skills than barely experienced United States male managers who participated in the study. This difference is presented in Table 38 and Figure 38 below.

Table 38

The Difference between Reported use of Intuition score of Male managers in Hong Kong with more than 20 years management experience and US male managers with 5 years or less management experience.

Variable	N	Minimum	Maximum	Mean	Std. Deviation
SCHK7	8	5	11	8.125	2.53193839
SCUS4	2	8	11	9.5	2.121320344

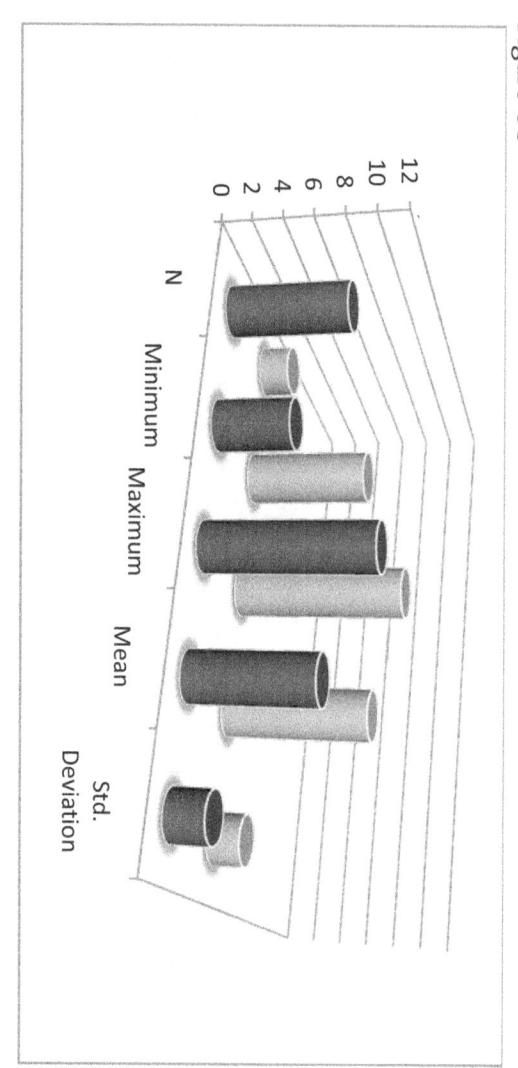

Figure 38

Finding 4.17: US male managers with over 20 years' use of intuition in decision making is higher than male managers in Hong Kong with between 11 and 20 years. Mean scores of US male managers with over 20 years is 7.1875; Male managers in Hong Kong with between 11 and 20 years is 6.8571. Significance is at the .025 level.

This finding show that well experienced US male managers who participated in the study used more intuitive right brain decision making skills than fairly experienced HK male managers who participated in the study. This difference is presented in Table 39 below.

Table 39

The Difference between Reported use of Intuition score of US male managers with over 20 years management experience and male managers in Hong Kong with between 11 and 20 years management experience.

Variable	N	Minimum	Maximum	Mean	Std. Deviation
SCUS7	16	4	10	7.1875	1.939716474
SCHK6	14	4	9	6.857142857	1.610405723

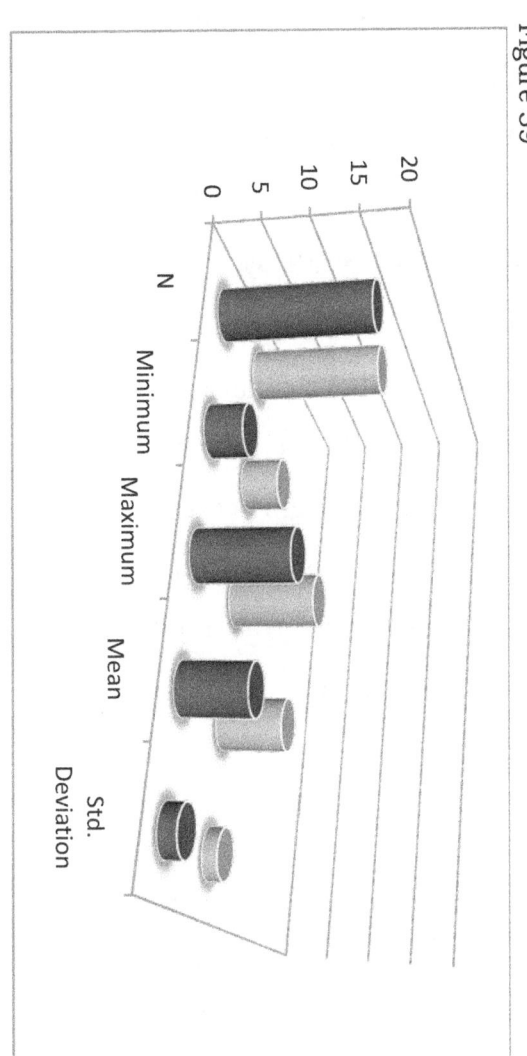

Figure 39

Finding 4.18: United States' female business owners' use of intuition in decision making is higher than Hong Kong female executives. Mean scores of US female business owners is 7.25; Hong Kong female executives is 6.307. Significance is at the .038 level.

This finding show that US female business owners who participated in the study used more intuitive right brain decision making skills than HK female executives who participated in the study. This difference is presented in Table 40 and Figure 40 below.

Half Brain Management Techniques 217

Table 40

The Difference between Reported use of Intuition score of US female business owners and Hong Kong female executives.

Variable	N	Minimum	Maximum	Mean	Std. Deviation
SCUS3	4	3	11	7.25	3.5
SCHK2	13	2	11	6.3076	2.92644

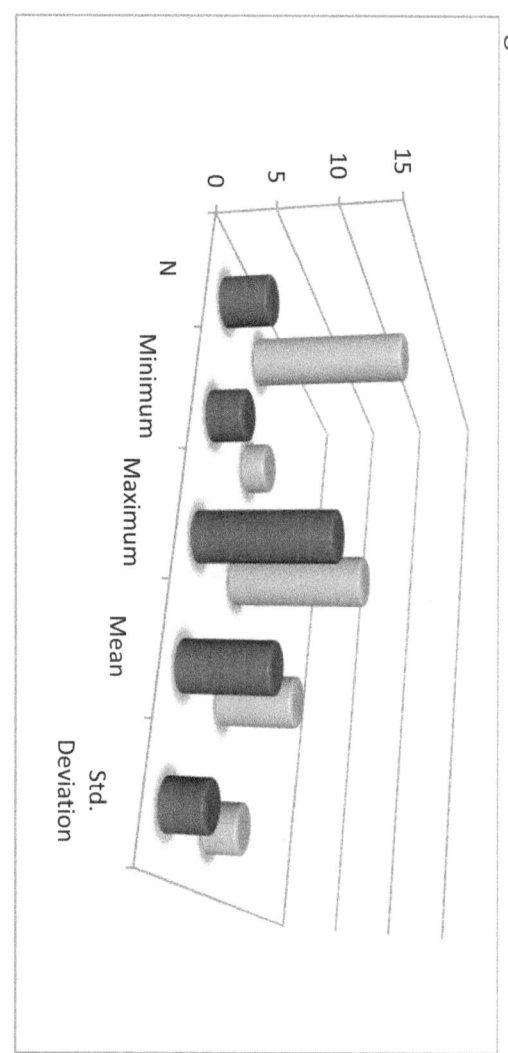

Figure 40

Finding 4.19: United States' business owners' use of intuition in decision making is lower than Hong Kong executives. Mean scores of US business owners is 7.0476; Hong Kong executives is 7.1785. Significance is at the .002 level.

This finding show that United States business owners who participated in the study used less intuitive right brain decision making skills than Hong Kong executives who participated in the study. This difference is presented in Table 41 and Figure 41 below.

Table 41

The Difference between Reported use of Intuition score of US business owners' and Hong Kong executives.

Variable	N	Minimum	Maximum	Mean	Std. Deviation
USSCO	21	3	11	7.0476	2.3340
HKSCS	28	2	11	7.1785	2.5539

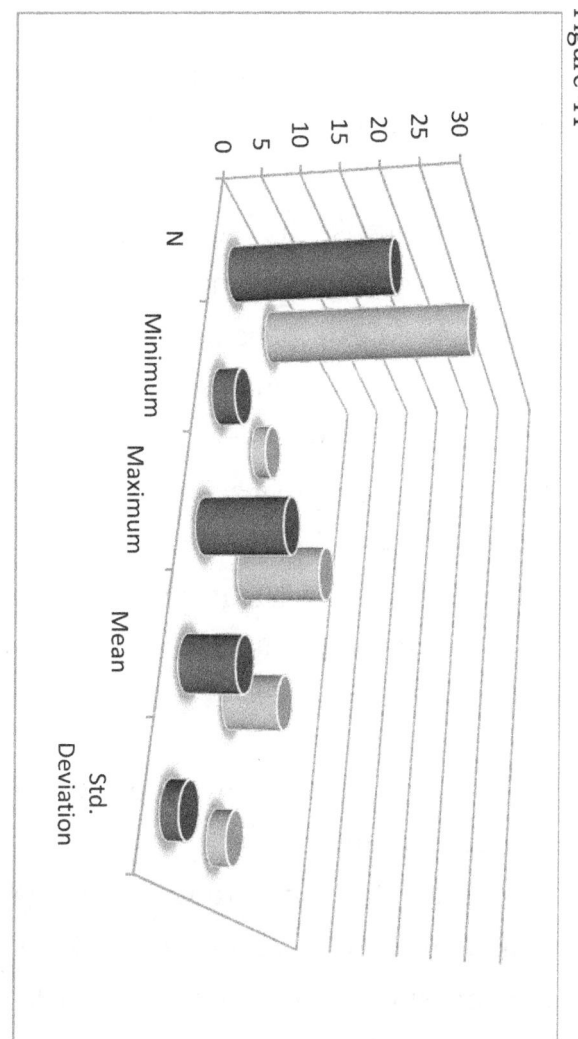

Figure 41

CONCLUSIONS AND RECOMMENDATIONS

President Barrack Obama reiterated what many management scholars have believed for years in his August 31st, 2010 speech; Innovation is the corner stone of United States' economy. If innovation is truly the cornerstone of the economy, why are management schools ignoring right-brain creative decision making techniques in their curriculum? Why are management schools reluctant to introduce right brain decision making techniques to their students? Why are business educators obdurate on teaching half brain management techniques?

Management education and practice as currently implemented can best be described as half brained. This comparative study has demonstrated the fact that managers across the board are still heavily dependent on left brain rational decision making despite the fact that studies show that most successful senior executives now utilize both sides of the brain to make decisions while at work.

Left brain rational managerial decision making currently emphasized in business schools remain half-brained regardless of how effective they think it is. Management education would never be regarded as full-brained until institutes begin to inculcate right brain decision making techniques into their curriculum and until then western management education would continue to be called half brain management education and the techniques taught by such institutes would remain half brain management techniques.

Recommendations

Based on the findings of this study, and current limited research, the following recommendations are proposed:

1. Continue studying the relationship between manager's genders, management levels, extents of management experience, and countries of operation and their reported uses of intuition in decision making.

2. Explore further what processes executives use to make effective decisions.

3. Research a smaller group of companies that agree to have management in different levels participate in the study.

4. Replicate this study in other countries.

5. Utilize awareness campaigns to remove secrecy surrounding the use of intuition in decision making.

REFERENCES CITED

A process for making good decisions (2005). *Iedex* Retrieved August 30, 2006 from http://www.iedex.com.au/essentials/html/d ecision_making.html

Agor, W.H. (1984). *Intuitive management: Integrating left and right brain management skills.* Englewood' s Cliffs, NJ: Prentice Hall.

Agor, W. H. (1986). *The logic of Intuitive decision-making: A research- based approach to top management.* New York: Quorum Books.

Agor, W. H. (1989). *Intuition in organizations: Leading and managing productively.* Newbury Park, CA: Sage.

Agor, W.H. (1991). *The logic of Intuition: How executives make important decisions: Intuition in organizations.* Newbury Park, CA: Sage Publications.

Atsunyo, M. (1992). *A comparative study of*

executive decision making in the United States and Ghana University of Massachusetts, Amherst, MA.

Ball D. A., McCulloh W.H., Frantz P.L., Geringer J.M. & Minor M.S. (2004) *International business: The challenge of global competition* New York, NY McGraw Hill/Irwin

Careerprospects.org (2006) Get ready to compete with workers in China, India, Africa & the rest of the world. *Career prospects in Virginia* Retrieved February, 2007 from http://www.careerprospects.org/Trends/ov erseas/Overseas.html

Cartwright T. (2004). *Developing your intuition: A guide to reflective practice* Greensboro, NC: Center for Creative Leadership.

Census.gov (2007) Trade deficit increases in 2006. *Frequently asked questions* Retrieved February, 2007 from http://www.census.gov/foreign-trade/www/

Church, M. J. (2005) Intuition, leadership, and decision making: A phenomenon *Dissertation Abstracts International,* 66(05), 1847. (UMI No. 3177390)

Cnet.com (2006) Cost of owning a hybrid. *Hybrid Car Buying Guide.* Retrieved from http://reviews.cnet.com/4520-10845_7-6212569-1.html?tag=lnav

Connor-Linton, J. (2003) Chi Square tutorial *Georgetown Linguistics* Retrieved August 15, 2006 from http://www.georgetown.edu/faculty/ballc/webtools/web_chi_tut.html

Damen, L. (1987). *Culture learning: The fifth dimension on the language classroom.* Reading, MA: Addison-Wesley.

Dowling P.J. & Welch D.E. (2005) *International human resource management* (4th ed.). Manson, Ohio: Thomson South-Western

Downey, L. (2006) Female intuition and emotional

intelligence linked to management success *Swinburne industry solutions* Retrieved December, 2006 from http://www.swinburne.edu.au/corporate/in dustrysolutions//newsArchive/news2006/a ugust/femaleIntui.htm

Drucker, P. F. (1967). The effective decision [Electronic version] *Management Review*, 56, 52-55

Drucker, P. F. (2004). What makes an effective executive? [Electronic version] *Harvard Business Review*, 82, 58-63

Drucker, P. F. (2007). *Management: Tasks, responsibilities, practices* New York, NY Harper Collins Publishers

Easton V. J. & McColl J.H. (n. d.) Statistics definitions *Statistics glossary* Retrieved August 15, 2006 from http://www.cas.lancs.ac.uk/glossary_v1.1/h yptest.html

Ebert R.J. & Griffin R. W. (2005) *Business Essentials* Upper Saddle River, New Jersey Pearson Prentice Hall

Familoni, O. J. (2003) Dream homes: Intuition, the hidden intelligence: factors that influence intuition in decision making of leaders from Nigeria and the United States *Dissertation Abstracts International*, 67(01), 582. (UMI No. 3069963)

Fan, P. & Zigang, Z. (2004) Cross-cultural challenges when doing business in China *Singapore Management Review* 26, 81-91

Fields A. F. (2003) A Study of Intuition in Decision-Making using Organizational Engineering Methodology. *Dissertation Abstracts International*, 66 (07), 2474. (UMI No. 3182016)

Firoz, N. M. (2002) Think globally manage culturally *International Journal of Commerce and Management* Retrieved August 12, 2006 from

http://goliath.ecnext.com/coms2/summary
_0199-480945_ITM

Follett, M. P. (1998). *The new state: Group organization the solution of popular government.* Pennsylvania Park: Pennsylvania State University Press. New York: Longman,

Golub A. L., (1997) *Decision Analysis: An Integrated Approach* Canada; John Wiley & Sons

Grace S. (2006) Spending in U.S. Telecommunications industry rises 8.9% in 2005 reaching $856.9 billion *Tiaonline.org* Retrieved August 15, 2006 from http://www.tiaonline.org/business/media/press_releases/2006/PR06-14.cfm

Headd B. (2005). Frequently asked questions S.B.A. office of advocacy Retrieved February, 2007 from http://www.sba.gov/advo/stats/sbfaq.pdf

Hksmea.asiansources.com. (2007) About the

association *Hong Kong small and medium enterprise association* Retrieved February, 2007 from http://hksmea.asiansources.com/

Hodgetts R.M., Luthans F., & Doh J.P. (2006) *International management: Culture, strategy and behavior* New York, NY McGraw Hill/Irwin

Hofstede, G. (2003) Geert Hofstede cultural dimensions *Itim International* Retrieved August 10, 2006 from http://www.geert-hofstede.com/hofstede_china.shtml

Isaack, T.S. (1978). Intuition: An ignored dimension of management *Academy of Management Review* 3, 917-922

Isenberg, D. (1984). How senior managers think. *Harvard Business Review*, 62, 81-90.

John M. & Taylor, P. S. (2006) Intuitive inventor, angelic writer *Washingtontimes.com* Retrieved September 18, 2006 from

http://washingtontimes.com/books/20060
916-112426-8471r.htm

Kasian, S. J. (2006) Dream homes: When
dreams seem to predict real estate sales.
Dissertation Abstracts International,
67(01), 582. (UMI No. 3205395)

Keegan, G. (2003) Glossary of Psychological terms
Gerard Keegan and his Psychology
Retrieved August 30, 2006 from
http://www.gerardkeegan.co.uk/glossary/
gloss_repwrit.htm

Kyle, B. (2002) *How Much for just the Spider?*
*Strategic web site marketing for small-
budget businesses* Bangor, ME:
Booklocker.com

Lau, D.C. (1992). The Analects by Confucius
Angelfire.com Retrieved October 02, 2006
http://www.angelfire.com/ego/nolimitz/con
fucius/analects.html

Lovell, J. (2001). The proverbs of a culture
reflect much of its attitudes.

Bigpond.net.au Retrieved August 10, 2006 from http://users.bigpond.net.au/bwi28/pro/julie.html

McCarthy J. C. (2002) 3.3million US services jobs to go offshore. *Making leaders successful everyday* Retrieved February, 2007 from http://www.forrester.com/ER/Research/Bri ef/ Excerpt/0,1317,15900,FF.html

Morris D., (2004) The Hybrid Highway *Mother Jones* Retrieved from http://www.motherjones.com/comment ary/columns/2004/02/02_204.html

Neidhardt W. J. (1984). The participatory nature of modern science and Judaic-Christian theism *Journal of the American Statistical Association* 36, 98-104

Nmsdcus.org (2007). Who we are *National minority supplier development council* Retrieved February, 2007 from http://www.nmsdcus.org

Power D.J. (2000). Supporting Decision-Makers: An Expanded Framework *DSSResources.COM* Retrieved from http://dssresources.com/papers/supportingdm/sld001.htm

Power D.J. (2004). Decision Support Systems Web Tour *dssresources.com* Retrieved from http://dssresources.com/tour/index.htm l

Prahlad, A. (2001) *Reggae wisdom: Proverbs in Jamaican music.* Jackson, MS: University ' Press of Mississippi

Richman M. (2002). The power of intuition *Interviews with James Wanless* Retrieved September 10, 2006 from http://www.jameswanless.info/interviews.ht ml

Robbins, S. P. (2004) *Organizational behavior* (11th ed.). Upper Saddle River, N.J: Prentice Hall.

Robbins, S. P., & Judge T.A. (2007) *Organizational behavior* (12th ed.). Upper Saddle River, New Delhi: Prentice Hall of India.

Robinson A. D. (1997). Intuition: A critical leadership skill [Electronic version] *Innovative Leader* 6, 251-300.

Salk J. (2005). An interview with Jonas Salk *Academy of achievement* Retrieved September 12, 2006 from http://www.achievement.org/autodoc/print member/sal0int-1

Sba.gov (2005) Frequently asked questions Retrieved January, 2007 from http://usinfo.state.gov/infousa/economy/in dustry/docs/sbfaq.pdf

Simon, H. A. (1987). Making management decisions: The role of intuition and emotion *The Academy of Management Executive*, 1, 57- 65

Surveysystem.com (2005) Sample size calculator *The survey system* Retrieved August 10, 2006 from http://www.surveysystem.com/sscalc.ht m

Uspto.gov (2006) U.S. Patent Statistics Chart Calendar Years 1963 – 2005 *PTMB reports* Retrieved January, 2007 from http://www.uspto.gov/go/oeip/taf/us_stat. htm

Wheelen, T. L., & Hunger J.D. (2004) *Strategic management and business policy* (9th ed.). Upper Saddle River, New Jersey: Pearson Prentice Hall.

Whiting, C.C. (2005) Intuitive decision-making and leadership style among healthcare executives in the United States. *Dissertation Abstracts International,* 66 (07), 2474. (UMI No. 3182016)

Wong P. T. (2006) Intuition: The best kept secret for survival and success *International network on personal meaning* Retrieved

October 10, 2006 from http://www.meaning.ca/articles06/presiden t/intuition-jun06.htm

APPENDICES

Appendix A: Intuitive Skill Survey

Thanks for participating in this academic survey. The survey is a test of intuitive skills. As soon as your survey is completed, we will send you the score. The score will show how you make decisions. Some people are more intuitive in making decisions while others are more rational. Intuitive decision making is not currently encouraged in many colleges, but studies showed that intuitive skills can translate into big money in your pocket. Most inventors are intuitive in their decision making and Thomas Edison (inventor of the light bulb) was one of them. Knowing your score can help you focus on the appropriate strategies to balance your decision making skills and as mentioned earlier, this can translate into big financial rewards in the future. Most successful business executives are intuitive decision makers. Please feel free to share this survey with your friends and family members; we welcome as many participants as possible. The survey will take about 10 minutes to complete.

Appendix B: Permission Letter to Use AIM Survey

Tuesday, February 6, 2007 10:45 AM

Dear Isola,

Thank you for sending the additional information. Please consider this written permission to reprint material as you have detailed below. Please include proper attribution to the original source. This permission does not extend to any 3rd party material found within our text. Please contact us for any future usage of the material.

Best,

Karen

Karen Wiley

Permissions Supervisor

Sage Publications, Inc.

2455 Teller Road

Thousand Oaks, CA 91320-2218

Phone: (805) 499-0721, Ext. 7735

Fax: (805) 499-0871

www.sagepub.com

From: OLuwabusuyi Isola

[mailto:oluwabusuyi5@yahoo.com]

Sent: Friday, January 19, 2007 9:31 PM

To: permissions

Subject: RE: AIM

Dear Karen,

Thanks, I hope the following information will help solve the problem.

Agor H. Weston (1989) *Intuition in Organizations: Leading and Managing Productively* Sage Publications, Inc The International Professional Publishers Newbury Park London New Delhi Page 134-139 ISBN 0803935633

Regards

Isola

permissions <permissions@sagepub.com> wrote:

Dear Isola,

Thank you for your request. Could you please sent full citation of the material you wish to reprint? We'll need to know the full source.

Best,

Karen

Karen Wiley

Permissions Supervisor

Sage Publications, Inc.

2455 Teller Road

Thousand Oaks, CA 91320-2218

Phone: (805) 499-0721, Ext. 7735

Fax: (805) 499-0871

www.sagepub.com

From: Oluwabusuyi Isola

[mailto:oluwabusuyi5@yahoo.com]

Sent: Tuesday, January 02, 2007 12:21 PM

To: permissions

Subject: AIM

Dear Sir/Ma,

I hereby ask for permission to reproduce the AIM
survey by Dr. Weston
H. Agor for my Doctoral dissertation at Argosy
University.

Regards

Isola

www.ingramcontent.com/pod-product-compliance
Lightning Source LLC
Chambersburg PA
CBHW071411170526
45165CB00001B/240